ALIN-KYAN

The Manual of Light

&

VIJJĀMAGGA DĪPANĪ

The Manual of the Path to Higher Knowledge

ALIN-KYAN

The Manual of Light

&

VIJJĀMAGGA DĪPANĪ

The Manual of the Path to Higher Knowledge

Two Expositions of the Buddha's Teaching

by

Ledi Sayādaw

Aggamahāpaṇḍita, D. Litt.

BPE

BPS Pariyatti Editions

BPS Pariyatti Editions
An imprint of Pariyatti Publishing
www.pariyatti.org

Published by Buddhist Publication Society, Kandy, Sri Lanka, 2008

Published with the consent of the original publisher.

First BPS Pariyatti Edition, 2018
ISBN: 978-1-68172-302-0 (Print)
ISBN: 978-1-68172-119-4 (PDF)
ISBN: 978-1-68172-117-0 (ePub)
ISBN: 978-1-68172-118-7 (Mobi)
LCCN: 2017919478

Contents

Publisher's Foreword to the American Edition

In recent years, many people in the West have been exposed to the teachings of the Buddha through the practice of Vipassana meditation as taught by S.N. Goenka. Mr. Goenka was born in Burma (now Myanmar) where he learned this technique of meditation from Sayagyi U Ba Khin, who had in turn been taught by Saya Thetgyi. Saya Thetgyi had the fortune to learn Vipassana from the highly respected scholar and meditator monk Ledi Sayādaw.

In Burma, Ledi Sayādaw is well known, and in his lifetime was the author of more than 100 books that provided both clarification and inspiration regarding the teachings of the Buddha. As Vipassana meditation in the tradition of Ledi Sayādaw begins to spread in the West, we are fortunate to begin to gain broader access to his writings as well.

We are grateful to the Buddhist Publication Society of Sri Lanka for allowing us to co-publish *The Manual of Light and The Manual of the Path to Higher Knowledge*. It is our sincere wish that this publication will prove valuable to those interested in understanding the Buddha's teaching at a deeper level, while providing the inspiration to continue walking step-by-step on the path.

Editor's Foreword to Alin-Kyan

In the *Manuals of Buddhism* (first published in 1965), there is reference to a translation, by the editors of the *Light of the Dhamma*, of the first two Chapters of *Alin-Kyan*, the *Manual of the Five Kinds of Light*. It has always been thought essential and long overdue that this work of Ledi Sayādaw should be readily available in a complete translation. Fortunately, a well-known translator, U Tin U (Myaung), skilfully produced an entirely new and readable translation in 1983. Due to a series of unfortunate difficulties and delays, it is only now that its publication has become possible.

With prior approval, the translation was submitted to the well-known Burmese scholar-monk Venerable Sayādaw U Ñāṇika Aggamahāpaṇḍita, who suggested several valuable improvements on the rendering of some technical Abhidhamma terms, as well as of a few Burmese words, most of which have now been incorporated in this first complete translation into English.

Venerable Ledi Sayādaw wrote the *Alin-Kyan* in Burmese, but he included many Pāḷi words. The retention of the Pāḷi in translations has always been considered essential, for, in case any doubt should arise as to the suitability of the word or words used by the translator, one can refer to the Pāḷi to find the exact meaning.

I do not think it would be out-of-place to repeat here what has already been said about the author in the Editor's Foreword to the English translation of the *Maggaṅga Dīpanī, The Manual of the Constituents of the Noble Path*:

> "Venerable Ledi *Araññavihāravāsī Mahā Thera* of Monywa, better known as the Venerable Ledi Sayādaw, *Aggamahāpaṇḍita*, *D. Litt.*, is described, in the short biography reproduced at the end of this work, as "perhaps the outstanding Buddhist figure of this age."

Of this there can be little doubt, and it is the reason why every attempt should be made to make known to Western readers, and in particular English-speaking readers, as many as possible of the numerous works originally written by him either in Pāḷi or Burmese, which are clear and precise expositions of Buddhism, suited to people of differing abilities and understanding, and invaluable aids for the study and practice of the Dhamma in all its aspects.

Of the works already translated into English, every credit must be given to the Pali Text Society, England, for publishing, as early as 1913–14, in their *Journal of the Pali Text Society* for those years, a translation of selected passages of *Yamaka Pucchā Vissajjanā*, "Some Points in Buddhist Doctrine," and in their Journal for 1915–16, a translation, by U Shwe Zan Aung, B.A., of *Paṭṭhānuddesa Dīpanī*, "Philosophy of Relations."

It is to Burma, however, that so much is owed for the translation into English and publication of the works of this Sayādaw in *The Light of the Dhamma*, the journal printed by the Union Buddha Sāsana Council Press. From its inception in 1952 until it ceased publication in 1963, *The Light of the Dhamma* published in serial form seven major works, translated by various hands. These *Dīpanīs* were combined into one volume, *The Manuals of Buddhism*, which was published by the Department of Religious Affairs, Rangoon.

Although the short biography included in this volume lists more than seventy works written by the Venerable Sayādaw, the final figure may well be found to be in excess of a hundred as further research continues and an attempt is made to compile a comprehensive list, including smaller articles not yet recorded, many relevant letters, etc. In addition, two biographies have been written in Burmese, but have not yet been translated into English.

A large number of Ledi Sayādaw's works are kept in the British Library in London. Every effort must be made to make as many as possible of the Sayādaw's other works, in Pāḷi, in Burmese, or in translation, accessible to the West by adding them, by way of presentation, to the large number of his works already held by the British Library in London, where they would continue to be available to bhikkhus, scholars, students and the like.

In undertaking the printing of the *Alin-Kyan*, however, a small effort is being made to make this fundamental exposition of the Buddha's Teaching available to interested students and readers in both the East and the West with the earnest wish that others will be encouraged thereby to help make the works of the Venerable Ledi Sayādaw known to a wider audience.

In addition to the invaluable aid it provides for students and other interested readers as a means of reference for purposes of study, the inclusion of Pāḷi may also be said to add to the translation the savour of the language of the Buddha himself, as found in the Pāḷi Canon, together with the voice of elucidation of its commentators.

S. S. Davidson, Southsea, 2001

The Manual of Light

Alin-Kyan

Namo Tassa Bhagavato Arahato Sammā Sambuddhassa

Veneration to the Exalted One, the Worthy One,
the Supremely Enlightened One

Chapter One

Five Kinds of Stark Ignorance and Five Kinds of Light

The Five Kinds of Stark Ignorance

1. Stark ignorance of *kamma* (*kamma-sammoha*)
2. Stark ignorance of the Dhamma (*dhamma-sammoha*)
3. Stark ignorance of causality (*paccaya-sammoha*)
4. Stark ignorance of the three characteristics of existence (*lakkhaṇa-sammoha*)
5. Stark ignorance of Nibbāna (*nibbāna-sammoha*)

The Five Kinds of Light

1. Knowledge in seeing that all beings have only *kamma* as their own property (*kammassakatā-ñaṇa*)
2. Knowledge in comprehending the Dhamma (*dhamma-vavatthāna-ñāṇa*)
3. Knowledge in comprehending the law of causality (*paccaya-vavatthāna-ñāṇa*)
4. Knowledge in realizing the three characteristics of existence (*lakkhaṇa-paṭivedha-ñāṇa*)
5. Knowledge in realizing Nibbāna (*nibbāna-paṭivedha-ñāṇa*)

Stark Ignorance of *Kamma*

Of these, *ignorance of kamma* (*kamma-sammoha*) means:

(i) Not understanding *kamma*
(ii) Not understanding the result of *kamma*

(i) *Not understanding kamma* means:

(a) Not understanding the fact that all beings have only *kamma* as their own property; that they must inherit their own *kamma*; that *kamma* alone is their origin; that *kamma* alone is their real relative; and that *kamma* alone is their real refuge.

(b) Not understanding which of their actions—bodily, verbal, or mental—are unwholesome, i.e., kammically unprofitable (*akusala*).

(c) Not understanding the fact that unwholesome actions bring unwholesome results in their future births, and will cast them down into the four lower worlds of unfortunate existences (*apāya*).

(d) Not understanding which of their actions—bodily, verbal, or mental—are wholesome, i.e., kammically profitable (*kusala*).

(e) Not understanding the fact that wholesome actions bring wholesome results in their future births, and will send them to fortunate existences in the human world or in the world of devas.

(ii) *Not understanding the result of kamma* means:

(a) Not understanding the fact that the lives of beings do not end at their biological death, but that they will arise in another existence where their *kamma* casts them, sends them, drags them, assigns them, or places them.

(b) Not understanding the fact that there exist an infinite number of sentient beings—though not visible to the naked eye—those in the tortuous worlds of hells (*niraya*), hungry spirits (*peta*), fallen spirits (*asurakāyas*), and animals.

(c) Not understanding the fact that, if they commit unwholesome acts, they are liable to be born in the four lower worlds (*apāya*) after their death.

(d) Not understanding the fact that there exist infinite numbers and types of human beings, visible to the ordinary human eye, as well as an infinite number of spirits and *devas*, good or bad, inhabiting the six *deva-lokas* (deva-worlds) and, higher up, the *brahmā-lokas* (brahma-worlds) of the fine material realms (*rūpī-brahmā*) and non-material realms (*arūpa-brahmā*).

(e) Not understanding the fact that through acquisition of merit by generosity (*dāna*), virtue or morality (*sīla*), and developing concentration (*bhāvanā*), beings are bound to be born in the fortunate planes of the human world and the celestial realms of *devas* and *brahmās*.

(f) Not understanding the existence of the round of births (*saṃsāra*), which is beginningless and endless.

(g) Not understanding the fact that all beings are subject to good or bad future births according to their own acts, whether good or bad, and that beings are born from existence to existence, incessantly, according to their own *kamma*.

Failure to understand all these things is called stark ignorance of *kamma* (*kamma-sammoha*).

Here ends the brief exposition of the first stark ignorance.

The First Light: Knowledge of *Kamma* Ownership

"Knowledge of *kamma* ownership" or "knowledge in seeing that all beings have *kamma* as their own property" (*kammas-sakatā-ñāṇa*),[1] means:

(i) Understanding *kamma*.

(ii) Understanding the result of *kamma*.

Understanding *kamma* and its result, means:

(a) Understanding the fact that all beings have only *kamma* as their own property; that they must inherit their own *kamma*; that *kamma* alone is their real relative; and that *kamma* alone is their real refuge.

(b) Understanding which of their actions—bodily, verbal, or mental—are unwholesome i.e., kammically unprofitable and will bring unwholesome results in their future births, casting them down into the four lower worlds.

(c) Understanding which of their actions are wholesome, i.e., kammically profitable and will bring wholesome results in their future births, sending them to fortunate existences in the human world and in the world of devas.

Understanding all these things is called knowledge of *kamma* ownership.

Here ends the brief exposition on the knowledge of kamma ownership.

Detailed Exposition on the Knowledge of *Kamma* Ownership

Dreadful indeed is stark ignorance of *kamma*. All sorts of wrong views (*micchā-diṭṭhi*) stem from it. Knowledge of *kamma* ownership on the other hand is the refuge for wayfarers in *sasra*, the beginningless round of births. It is only under the guidance of this light that beings perform such meritorious deeds as giving, observance of morality, and the practice of mental concentration, and attain successful existences as men, *devas*, or *brahmās*. It is this light that enables one to practise wholesome deeds to the perfection (*pāramī-kusala*) that is the prerequisite for enlightenment, such as the Perfect Self-Enlightenment of a Buddha, the solitary self-enlightenment of a Paccekabuddha, or the arahatship of a Noble Disciple (*sāvaka-bodhi*).

The light of the knowledge of *kamma* ownership exists in those men and *devas* in the innumerable universes or world systems who have right view (*sammā-diṭṭhi*). In our universe, too, even during an empty world cycle when the world is without the benefit of any Buddha, this light exists. By right view (*sammā-diṭṭhi*), of course, we mean this light of the knowledge of *kamma* ownership.

At the present time, this light prevails among the Buddhists and Hindus in the world. Among people of other creeds and among animals, this light does not exist. Few among the inhabitants of the tortuous realm of *niraya*, the realm of the fallen spirits (*asūrakāya*), and the realm of the hungry spirits (*peta*) have the benefit of this light. Those beings who do not possess such light dwell in the darkness of *kamma-sammoha*. As they are enveloped in stark ignorance, the path leading to successful existences in the round of births is lost to them. Being incapable of lifting themselves up to the fortunate planes of human, *deva*, or *brahmā* existences, they are destined to go down to the lower worlds, whose portals are ever wide open. For these beings, thousands, tens of thousands, or hundreds of thousands of existences may pass without their ever getting the slightest benefit of this beneficent light.

Only in the case of a confirmed Buddha-to-be (*bodhisatta*) who has obtained the word of assurance from a living Buddha about his future Buddhahood, has the shroud of ignorance been lifted, so that, even when born an animal, he is still endowed with this light. This light belongs to the holders of right view, even during the world-cycles (*kappa*) devoid of any Buddha and in those universes that lack the benefit of a Buddha's arising. Buddhas do not arise in the world only to expound this light, but to expound the light of knowledge that penetrates the Four Noble Truths (*catusacca-paṭivedha-ñāṇa*). Therefore, the light of knowledge of *kamma* ownership cannot be called a light of the Buddha's Teaching—in spite of its mention in many Buddhist scriptures. It is merely a worldly light, a light that does not shed its rays beyond *saṃsāra*.

People who have the benefit of the Buddha's Teaching, therefore, if they are wise enough, will not remain satisfied merely with the light of knowledge of *kamma* ownership, but will rouse themselves to acquire the true light of the Buddha's Teaching. This is indeed is the wise course.

Here ends the exposition of the first pair—stark ignorance of kamma and the first light.

Stark Ignorance of the Dhamma

Ignorance of the *Dhamma* (*dhamma-sammoha*) means:

1. Not understanding the Dhamma as the Dhamma.
2. Not understanding the ultimate truth about existence in what is generally taken as person (*puggala*), being (*satta*), self or soul (*attā*), or life (*jīva*), which is, in truth and reality, the mere compounded existence of materiality and mentality or mind and matter (*nāma-rūpa*) comprising the five aggregates.

The Three Perversions

Out of this stark ignorance of the Dhamma, there spring the three perversions (*vipallāsa*), namely: (a) perverted perception (*saññā-vipallāsa*), (b) perverted consciousness (*citta-vipallāsa*), and (c) perverted view (*diṭṭhi-vipallāsa*).

(a) Perverted perception means having wrong perceptions about things; for example, mere phenomena (*dhammā*) are not perceived as mere phenomena, but as a person, a being, a self (soul), a life, a woman, or a man, etc.

(b) Perverted consciousness means the inability to think of phenomena as mere phenomena, but thinking of them in terms of a person, a being, a self (soul), a life, a woman, or a man, etc.

(c) Perverted view means taking a wrong, perverted view of things; for example, not seeing mere phenomena as mere phenomena, but taking them for granted, through convention, as a person, a being, a self (or soul), a life, a woman, or a man, etc.

These are the three errors arising from stark ignorance of the Dhamma, and out of these three errors, there grow ten kinds of misdeeds, such as killing living beings. Wrong views and all sorts of consequent evil grow as well.

The Second Light: Knowledge in Comprehending the Dhamma

Knowledge in comprehending the Dhamma[2] (*dhamma-vavatthāna-ñāṇa*) means:

1. Clear understanding that in the entire world no such thing as a person, a being, a self (soul), or a life, a woman, or a man really exists, but only mere phenomena (*dhammā*), mind-and-matter, or mentality-materiality (*namā-rūpa*).
2. Perceiving the distinction between physical phenomena (*rūpa*) and mental phenomena (*nāma*).
3. Perceiving the distinction between one physical phenomenon and another physical phenomenon.
4. Perceiving the distinction between one mental phenomenon and another mental phenomenon.

It means, in brief, the whole thing amounts to right view (*sammā-diṭṭhi*), which also goes by the name of purification of view (*diṭṭhi-visuddhi*).

Dreadful indeed is the stark ignorance of the Dhamma. It is only with the golden opportunity of coming under the Buddha's Teaching that we can gain the clear understanding that mentality-materiality, a composite of the five aggregates of existence, are, in ultimate truth, mere phenomena (*suddha-dhammā*). Without the benefit of the Buddha's Teaching, beings may pass from one existence to another a hundred times, a thousand times, tens of thousands of times, or an infinite number of times (*asaṅkheyya*), and yet no such knowledge can dawn on them. This is the light that only the Buddha's Teaching can provide.

Even at present, when the golden opportunity of the Buddha's Teaching is available, there are multitudes who, not realizing phenomena as mere phenomena, not understanding materiality as mere materiality, and not understanding mentality as mere mentality, are shrouded by this dreadful stark ignorance of the Dhamma. They remain helpless in stark darkness. Lacking this light, their existence is marked by a proliferation of the three perversions, the ten kinds of misdeeds, all kinds of wrong views, and consequent evils. Release from the rigorous round of births is not in sight for them. Indeed, they are heading straight for the whirlpool of *saṃsāra* to drift, sink, and drown. Therefore, it is appropriate for the wise and wary to strive to understand the phenomena of mentality-materiality, and to gain analytical insight.

Here ends the exposition of the second pair—stark ignorance of the Dhamma and the second light.

The Stark Ignorance of Causality

Ignorance of causality (*paccaya-sammoha*) means:

1. Not understanding the origin of mentality-materiality.
2. Not understanding the twelve constituents (*aṅga*) that make up the law of dependent origination (*paṭicca-samuppāda*) as declared by the Buddha: "With ignorance (*avijjā*) as condition, there arise volitional activities (*saṅkhārā*); with volitional activities as condition, there arises consciousness (*viññāṇa*); with consciousness as condition, there arises mentality-materiality (*nāma-rūpa*); ... the six sense-bases (*saḷāyatana*); ... contact (*phassa*); ... feeling (*vedanā*); ... craving (*taṇhā*); ... clinging (*upādāna*); ... the process of becoming (*bhava*); birth (*jāti*); ... ageing and death (*jarā-maraṇa*), sorrow (*soka*), lamentation (*parideva*), suffering or pain (*dukkha*), grief (*domanassa*), and despair (*upāyāsa*). Thus, there arises this 'whole mass of suffering' (*dukkhakkhandha*)."

When one is ignorant of this law of causality, one firmly holds the "wrong view that there is a doer" (*kāraka-diṭṭhi*), insisting that if there is an action there is a doer, so that mentality-materiality cannot be seen as distinct phenomena (*dhammā*), but as some person or being.

The Third Light: Knowledge in Comprehending the Law of Causality

Knowledge in comprehending the law of causality (*paccaya-vavatthāna-ñāṇa*) means:

1. Understanding the origin of mentality-materiality.
2. Understanding the twelve constituents (*aṅgā*) that make up the law of dependent origination as declared by the Buddha thus: "With ignorance as condition, there arise volitional activities; ... Thus there arises this 'whole mass of suffering'."

Three Kinds of Grave Wrong Views

Out of stark ignorance of causality, three kinds of grave wrong views arise, namely: (1) the wrong view of no-cause (*ahetuka-diṭṭhi*); (2) the wrong view that the world is created by an eternal God (*visamahetu-diṭṭhi*); (3) the wrong view that the world is a product of past deeds (*pubbekata-hetu-diṭṭhi*).

1. The wrong view of no-cause holds that all phenomena in the world, both mental and physical, arise through no cause, exist through no cause, and happen by mere chance.
2. The wrong view that the world is created by an eternal God believes in a cause, but assigns the cause to an omnipotent creator, an eternal God, or providence. All beings, all physical and mental phenomena, all things, all activities, and all happenings are in accordance with this God. This is, in fact, baseless, untenable, uneven, and unjust.
3. The wrong view that the world is a product of past deeds believes in reasoned cause and, while rejecting the theory of a creator, accepts the view that the world (i.e., all mentality-materiality) arises and is conditioned by wholesome and unwholesome actions done by beings in their past existences. This view takes into account only past *kamma*, in total disregard of present volitional activities.

Of these three wrong views, the first and second are gross views. The third, being partially correct, is relatively less erroneous.

Why the Wrong View of No-Cause is Partially Right

Mentality-materiality is conditioned by:

(a) Past *kamma.*
(b) Present consciousness (*citta*).
(c) Temperature prevailing at present (*utu*).
(d) Nutriment in the present life (*āhāra*).

That being so, this view is correct insofar as it relates to mentality-materiality which arises on account of past *kamma*; but, as regards all other mentality-materiality caused by consciousness, temperature, or nutriment, it is wrong.

If we apply the law of dependent origination, this view holds good for those factors which are conditioned by past *kamma*, but it is wrong in respect of those which are themselves the present causes, i.e., the conditions for rebirth-linking in the future, namely, ignorance, volitional activities, craving, clinging, and the process of becoming.

If we consider it in the light of the Paṭṭhāna's doctrine of the twenty-four relations, this view recognizes only the relationship of past *kamma* to its effects (*nānākkhaṇika-kamma-paccaya*) and rejects the twenty-three other relations, as well as the relation of co-nascent or coexistent *kamma* (*sahajāta-kamma-paccaya*). Thus, this view, while being partially right, is substantially wrong.

These three kinds of wrong view, together with all sorts of other wrong views and sceptical doubt (*vicikicchā*), spring from the stark ignorance of causality.

The Future Stream-Enterer

Understanding dependent origination or the law of causality enables one to discard the three wrong views of no-cause, a creator God, and past *kamma* alone. In fact, according to the commentaries, this knowledge equips one to be a future stream-enterer (*cūla-sotāpanna*),[3] a virtuous one, ever freed from the ignoble destinies of the four lower worlds. Hence this is a goal well worth striving for.

Here ends the exposition of the third pair—stark ignorance of causality and the third light.

Stark Ignorance of the Three Characteristics of Existence

Ignorance of the 'three' characteristics of existence (*lakkhaṇa-sammoha*) means the inability to understand the truth of the interrelatedness of the phenomena of mentality-materiality:

1. That they have the characteristic of impermanence (*anicca*), being in a rapid state of flux.
2. That they have the characteristic of suffering or pain (*dukkha*), very much to be dreaded.
3. That they have the characteristic of non-self (*anattā*) in the sense that they are mere conditioned phenomena lacking substance, essence, or life that can, in truth and reality, be called a person or a being.

The Fourth Light: Knowledge in Realizing the Three Characteristics of Existence

Knowledge in realizing the three characteristics of existence (*lakkhaṇa-paṭivedha-ñāṇa*) means realizing through insight the truth of the interrelatedness of the phenomena of mentality-materiality:

1. That they have the characteristic of impermanence (*anicca*), being in a rapid state of flux.
2. That they have the characteristic of suffering or pain (*dukkha*), very much to be dreaded.
3. That they have the characteristic of non-self (*anattā*) in the sense that they are mere conditioned phenomena lacking substance, essence, or life that can, in truth and reality, be called a person or a being.

It is this realization, this light, that enables the Buddha, the Paccekabuddhas, and the Arahats to gain release from the darkness of defilements (*kilesa*), the dungeon of fettered existence (*bhava*), and the stout bonds of craving (*taṇhā*) that bind all worldlings, keeping them hopelessly entangled, thereby exposing them forever to the perils and sufferings of *saṃsāra*.

Failing to realize the three characteristics, both bhikkhus and laypeople alike, fumble in the darkness of their own defilements, in their dungeon of fettered existence. Bound by stout bonds of craving, they get entangled and are forever exposed to the perils and sufferings of *saṃsāra*. Only when they attain the light of this knowledge do they dispel the darkness of stark ignorance of the three characteristics. Then, and only then, can they gain release from the bondage of their own craving and attain Nibbāna.

Here ends the exposition of the fourth pair—stark ignorance of the three characteristics and the fourth light.

Stark Ignorance of Nibbāna

Ignorance of Nibbāna (*nibbāna-sammoha*) may be briefly explained as follows.

As wayfarers in the woeful round of existences, most beings are ignorant of their true plight. They fail to understand the right practice by which they can bring about a complete cessation of all suffering (*dukkha*) through the cutting off of all fetters and entanglements of their own craving. They do not know that there is such a practice under the Buddha's Teaching that can save them from the darkness of defilements and, having stilled their burning desires, land them in the absolute peace (*santi*) which is Nibbāna.

The Fifth Light: Knowledge in Realizing Nibbāna

The five kinds of stark ignorance give way stage by stage to the five kinds of light. Once the fifth light is attained, the whole darkness of the five kinds of stark ignorance is completely dispelled. The total extinction of this whole mass of ignorance, with no possibility of its ever arising again, is the final goal of absolute peace, Nibbāna.

Furthermore, with the total extinction of the five kinds of stark ignorance, there also go to extinction the ten kinds of misdeeds, all forms of evil, all wrong views, and all misguided actions, thereby forever freeing one from the ignoble destinies of the four lower worlds.

Knowledge in realizing Nibbāna (*nibbāna-paṭivedha-ñāṇa*) is the full knowledge that such a worthy goal of peace or tranquillity exists and the realization of this peace through one's own experience. This fifth light is, in short, the four stages of enlightenment and the knowledge of the noble path.

Here ends the brief exposition of the five kinds of stark ignorance and the five kinds of light.

CHAPTER TWO

The Four Lights of the Buddha's Teaching

Of the five kinds of light, the first—knowledge in seeing that all beings have only *kamma* as their own property—is not actually a light of the Buddha's Teaching. It is merely a light available in *saṃsāra*, or a light available in the world, a worldly light.

Only the remaining four are truly the light of the Buddha's Teaching:

1. Knowledge in comprehending the Dhamma (*dhamma-vavatthāna-ñāṇa*)—the second light.
2. Knowledge in comprehending the law of causality (*paccaya-pariggaha* or *paccaya-paṭivedha-ñāṇa*)—the third light.
3. Knowledge in realizing the three characteristics of existence (*lakkhaṇa-paṭivedha-ñāṇa*)—the fourth light.
4. Knowledge in realizing Nibbāna (*nibbāna-paṭivedha-ñāṇa*)—the fifth light.

Therefore, in this second chapter, I shall not discuss the first light, but shall dwell on the four true lights of the Buddha's teaching in a fairly comprehensive manner.

The Six Elements and Ultimate Truth

To establish oneself in the Dhamma or to attain the light of knowledge in comprehending the Dhamma, it may properly be asked: "What is the absolute minimum one must understand about mentality-materiality in order to attain this second light?" The answer is understanding the six elements (*dhātu*), namely:

(1) The element of extension (*paṭhavī-dhātu*).
(2) The element of cohesion (*āpo-dhātu*).
(3) The element of heat (*tejo-dhātu*).
(4) The element of motion (*vāyo-dhātu*).
(5) The element of space (*ākāsa-dhātu*).
(6) The element of consciousness (*viññāṇa-dhātu*).

In worldly usage we speak of a person or being or a life but these are mere conceptual terms. In the ultimate sense, however, according to the Abhidhamma, there is no personal entity in what is generally called a person or a being—no soul, no self, nor a life anywhere. What really exists are the six elements mentioned above.

Let us take one example. We have around us a variety of structures built of timber or bamboo, such as a house, a monastery, a temple, a rest-house. When we speak of a certain structure as a "house," we are not referring to the timber or the bamboo of which it is built. Rather we are referring to a certain type of structure generally recognized as a house, which is only a secondary name of the timber or bamboo in it. When these materials—timber or bamboo—were in the form of standing trees, they were not called a house. Only when they have assumed the shape of a house do they acquire the secondary name of "house." Now, this name is a mere coinage, something that has suddenly appeared, like a bolt from the blue. It is actually foreign to the real material from which it is built. In the ultimate sense, therefore, we see that there is no such thing as "house," but only timber or bamboo.

The word "house," therefore, refers only to a certain type of structure, after it has taken on a certain shape or appearance; in the last analysis, it does not exist. The same materials—timber or bamboo, as the case may be—that went into the construction of the house may, after the house has been pulled down, be reused for a monastery. They then assume the form of a monastery, and are, accordingly, called a monastery. The shape and form of a house is no longer there, so we do not call it a house anymore. Again, let us say, those same materials, after the monastery has been pulled down, are reused for a temple or a turreted tower (*pyathat*) in front of a pagoda. Then they assume the new shape known as a temple or a turretted tower, and are, therefore, called a "temple," or a "tower," and not a "monastery." Further, let us say that these materials are reused in the construction of a rest-house. The name "temple" disappears and the new name of "rest-house" is used for the same materials. Further still, if that rest-house is converted into a monastery, the name "rest-house" disappears and a new name of "monastery" comes into use. When forms are destroyed, names disappear. Only when forms appear, do names also come into common usage.

The materials—timber or bamboo—that have gone into the construction of the various structures have remained just timber or bamboo. They were timber or bamboo as standing trees. When they assumed the various shapes of "house," "monastery," "temple," "rest-house," they were still timber or bamboo. When the rest-house is pulled down, and its component parts piled on the ground, the materials are still timber or bamboo. Originally, there was no such thing as a house, a monastery, a temple, a rest-house. Only when the basic materials are assembled into such shapes do those terms become valid. The basic materials, timber or bamboo, remain throughout timber or bamboo, as they were originally. Thus, in the ultimate sense, according to the Abhidhamma, there is no such thing as "house," "monastery," "temple," "rest-house"; in truth and reality, only timber or bamboo exists.

Nevertheless, when we say the house exists, we are not telling a falsehood, for in the conventional sense the statement is true, and it does not mislead anyone. In the ultimate sense of the Abhidhamma, however, it is wrong to say the house exists, because what we call a house is merely a certain structural form built by the architect, conventionally accepted as a house. If someone asks, "What actually is the thing called 'house'?" and someone else points to the building and says, "This is a house," in conventional usage this is correct. But in the Abhidhamma sense it is incorrect.

Why is that? Let us ask, "What is the finger actually pointing at?" The house or the timber or bamboo? Since what is called a house is in fact a mere structural form, what is actually being indicated is only the timber or bamboo, the real things, the things that existed originally. To call these materials a house is merely a misconception, a case of mistaken identity. If the name "house" was the true name that is intrinsically applicable to timber or bamboo, the name must have been used when timber or bamboo was standing as trees. And also, whatever form of structure (monastery, temple, etc.) these materials may have assumed, the name "house" should be the valid term of reference for them. But this is not the case. A house is a house only when certain materials are put into a certain conventional form called a "house." Similarly, the names "monastery," "temple," etc., also are valid only when the basic materials have the shapes of what are conventionally recognized as monastery, temple, etc. This is how conventional truth differs from the ultimate truth of the Abhidhamma. This difference should be well understood.

Of these two kinds of truth, conventional truth is used in the mundane sphere, and is valid only in its own sphere. The ultimate truth of the Abhidhamma, on the other hand, is useful to get one beyond the mundane sphere to the supramundane sphere of Nibbāna. Using timber or bamboo, we make all sorts of objects; for example, a couch, a throne, a bench, a boat, or a cart, which conventionally go by these various names. In the Abhidhamma sense, however, no such thing as couch, throne, bench, boat, or cart really exists; only the materials of which they are made really exist. Using earth, we make pots, basins, cups, and vessels, which are conventionally called by these respective names. According to the Abhidhamma, however, there are no such things as pots, basins, cups, or vessels; all are only earth. Iron is made into all sorts of ironware; copper into all sorts of copperware; gold into all sorts of gold ware; silver into all sorts of silverware; cotton into all sorts of fabrics and dresses; and all of them acquire the names of the fabricated products. According to the Abhidhamma, none of those objects exist; only the basic materials from which they are made exist. We must make a clear distinction between the original materials and the fabricated object that has taken on a certain form.

In respect to a person, a being, a self (soul), or a life, as well, these terms are valid only conventionally. In the Abhidhamma, there exists no person, no being, no self (soul), nor a life; only the six basic elements exist. In truth, no such thing as man or *deva, Sakka* or *Brahmā*, cow, buffalo, or elephant exists; in reality, in all the world, only the six basic elements exist. Woman, man, person, you, I, etc., are conventional terms for that which does not really exist. Only the six basic elements really exist. There is no head, leg, hand, eye, ear, nose, etc., because, in the last analysis, all are only the six basic elements. All the organs of the body, such as, hair, body-hair, nails, teeth, skin, flesh, sinews, bones, bone-marrow, kidneys, heart, liver, pleura, spleen, lungs, large intestines, small intestines, stomach, bowels (faeces), etc., do not exist; only the elements really exist.

All along the vast extent of *saṃsāra's* journey, we have become ingrained in misconceptions about things all around us, believing mere forms to be facts of life. The truth is that all things, big or small, in the ultimate analysis, are a mere heap of elements, a mass of elements, a collection of elements, a lump of elements, and nothing more. This definitive insight is the first light of the Buddha's Teaching, knowledge in comprehending the Dhamma (*dhamma-vavatthāna-ñāṇa*).

The Four Great Elements

Of the six elements, the four great elements are:

(1) Element of extension, or the earth element (*paṭhavī*).
(2) Element of cohesion, or the water element (*āpo*).
(3) Element of heat, or the fire element (*tejo*).
(4) Element of motion, or the wind element (*vāyo*).

Earth has the property of hardness (*kakkhaḷa*) or softness (*mudu*). This property is the earth element, in the ultimate sense.

Water has the property of cohesion (*ābandhana*) or liquidity (*paggharaṇa*). This property is the water element, in the ultimate sense.

Fire has the property of heat (*uṇhabhāva*) or cold (*sītabhāva*). This property is the fire element, in the ultimate sense.

Wind has the property of support (*vitthambhana*) or motion (*samudīraṇa*). This property is the wind element, in the ultimate sense.

The meaning of these four great elements should be digested and learned by heart.

I shall proceed to expound these four great elements, so that the light of knowledge in comprehending the Dhamma (*dhamma-vavatthāna-ñāṇa*) may dawn on the reader.

Analysis of the Earth Element

The earth element (*paṭhavī-dhātu*), in the ultimate sense, is the mere property of hardness. By earth is not meant any substance—not even a hundred-thousandth part of an atom. It lacks shape, mass, form, core, or solidity. Therefore, this element exists in very clear spring water or river water; in all forms of light, including sunlight, moonlight, and even the lustre of gems; in all sounds, including the vibrant sounds of gongs or pagoda bells; in moving air, from the softest breeze to a gale; and in smells, good or bad, that spread near and far.

The reason for this peculiar property lies in the state of inseparability (*avinibbhoga-vutti*) of the four great elements. For as the Buddha says:

"Depending on one of the great elements, the remaining three arise. Depending on three of them, the remaining one arises. Depending on two of them, the remaining two arise."

Ekaṃ mahābhūtaṃ paṭicca tayo mahābhūtā;
Tayo mahābhūte paṭicca ekaṃ mahābhūtaṃ;
Dve mahābhūte paṭicca dve mahābhūtā. (Paṭṭhāna I § 53)

The Commentaries explain that it is the function (*sampaṭicchana-rasā*) of the earth element to receive the three other co-nascent elements of water, wind, and fire.

The water, wind, and fire elements have a nature such that they cannot exist without the earth element as their basis.

Therefore, it should be understood that in all forms of water, colour, sound, wind, and smell, this earth element invariably exists.

This is on the authority of the scriptures. We can also prove its existence by empirical data. In any mass of water or wind, it is fairly evident that the lower layers are supporting the successively higher ones. This function of supporting is not the property of the water element, which is characterized by cohesion. It is not the property of heat either, for heat is characterized by its thermal quality only. Support is the joint function of the earth and wind elements. Support implies hardness or the capacity to bear, as well as lifting or the capacity to resist. The former is the property of the earth element; the latter is the property of the wind element. The wind element acquires its property of resistance on the strength of hardness, the property of the earth element. It cannot function alone. One should try to understand this distinction between hardness and resistance, both of which exist in the function of supporting.

Thus, we can discern the presence of hardness in water or in wind, and from that we can safely conclude that the earth element, the element of extension, which has the property of hardness, exists in water and wind.

In the case of light and smell, however, although the element of extension is definitely there, this element is too subtle to notice. No empirical data can be drawn from them. We simply have to rely on the authority of the scriptures.

The fact of the presence of the earth element in the clearest water, light, wind, sound, and smell, is stated here to impress upon you the truth that when we refer to the earth element, what we really mean is the mere property of hardness, and that the property of hardness does *not* refer to a particle that has any form, solidity, or substance, even as minute as the hundred thousandth part of an atom. The mere *property* of hardness must not be confused with the *manifestation* of hardness in things.

We should understand the term "hardness" as a relative concept. Something that is "hard" or "soft" has that characteristic in comparison to something else. Thus, there are varying degrees of hardness in that which we call softness. With the cutting diamond at one extreme and the corporeality of a moonbeam at the other, we can discern the same property of hardness in varying degrees in all materiality. That is the character of the earth element. This character of hardness can only be discerned as an ultimate truth. For, if conventional perception stands in the way, no "hardness" can ever be found in subtle materiality, such as moonlight.

When hundreds of thousands of crores of the earth element—by themselves the mere property of hardness—happen to be held together by the element of cohesion or the water element (*āpo-dhātu*), a form appears, which is given the name "atom." When thousands of crores of such atoms come together, certain forms of life come into being, beginning with tiny insects. As the materiality increases, all kinds of beings with varying sizes, up to the Lord of the Fallen Spirits (*asurinda*), whose height is 4,800 *yojanas,* take form. As regards external things, this phenomenon of materiality can assume a form as large as Mount Meru, which is 168,000 *yojanas* high, or even the Great Earth itself which has a thickness of 240,000 *yojanas*.

It is the earth element with its property of hardness that serves as the basis of all forms of materiality, animate or inanimate, from atoms and insects to the entire universe. No other element has the property of assuming form or shape. The three other elements of water, wind, and fire depend on earth for their existence. Thus, one must realize the importance of earth as the basic element in all materiality.

If you want to contemplate the earth element as an ultimate reality in Mount Meru or in this Great Earth, you concentrate only on the property of hardness, which lacks substance. As you concentrate only on its function (giving support to all forms of materiality) it will be seen as a reflection in a mirror or on the surface of clear water, without the obstruction of the tiniest substance, not even an atom.

If there remains the faintest idea of substance or form or solid mass, even as much as an atom, your view is not on the ultimate truth of earth. It is not free from the conventionally accepted concept of form. This conventional truth stands in the way of understanding the true characteristics—arising and vanishing—of materiality.

It should be mentioned here that when Venerable Puṇṇa instructed Venerable Ānanda on this subject of contemplating the elements, he used the example of the image in the mirror, and Venerable Ānanda attained the first stage of enlightenment as a stream-enterer (*sotāpanna*).

If one can clearly understand the property of hardness that truly exists in Mount Meru or the Great Earth, unencumbered by any conventional concept of substance or form, one should find it much easier to understand this ultimate truth in lesser objects, animate or inanimate.

Images reflected in a mirror—be they as big as Mount Meru—are liable to vanish in an instant, more than a hundred times shorter than the blink of an eye or a flash of lightning, because there is actually no trace of any substance in them. In exactly the same way, the earth element in all materiality—be it as big as Mount Meru—is liable to vanish in an instant just as short, because, in the ultimate sense, there is no substance, not even as much as an atom, in it. With practice and insight, the meditator will realize this truth. When contemplating the earth element in one's own body with a view to gaining insight into physical phenomena, the meditator should concentrate on one specific part at a time. When contemplating the earth element in the head, one should focus one's attention on all parts of the head, both inside and out. While doing so, the concept of colour, which is not a basic property of the earth element, might come in. The concept of form or shape might also stand in the way. Using great mental alertness, all these obstructive concepts must be discarded.

Proceeding to the lower parts of his body, down to the soles of the feet, the meditator should select each field of concentration to suit his own ability. After he has covered the whole body in this way, one part at a time, he will be able to contemplate the earth element in any part, for example the head, and, at the same time, be able to comprehend it within the whole body. Once such comprehension has arisen within oneself, one comprehends the same phenomenon in all other things, animate or inanimate, throughout the universe—indeed, even in other universes.

And once the earth element is thus comprehended, one finds no difficulty in comprehending the three remaining elements.

Here ends the brief analysis of the earth element.

Analysis of the Water Element

Water has the property of cohesion. The water element (*āpo-dhātu*) is, in the ultimate sense, the mere property of cohesion. When the property of cohesion is strong it tends to ooze and become fluid—hence the earth element is expressed as the water element. This basic property of cohesion, in the ultimate sense, bears no substance whatsoever, not even a hundred-thousandth part of an atom: it is just a property or a function. Its function is to bind together the three other coexisting elements of earth, fire, and wind, so that the four exist interdependently. Once the water element disappears, the three other elements disintegrate and vanish at once. This is the crucial function of the water element in any given group or unit of materiality.

All material shapes and forms, ranging from the atom to Asurinda, Lord of the Asuras, in the living world, as well as all physical phenomena up to Mount Meru and the Great Earth, exist in the world due to the water element. Apart from this water element, there is no other element which holds materiality together.

If cohesion were to fail in Mount Meru, the whole 168,000 *yojanas* of the great mountain would crumble and vanish in no time. The same would be true of Mount Cakkavāḷa, which is 164,000 *yojanas* high, or of the Great Earth, in which case we would have to imagine an eerie void in place of the Great Earth. This is because when the function of cohesion is absent, even the rock formations that make Mount Meru, Mount Cakkavāḷa, and the Great Earth cannot stand together since the primary elements that constitute them lack the necessary binding force.

All the elements, in the ultimate sense, with the exception of Nibbāna, have the nature of being formed or conditioned interdependently. They cannot exist for a moment, not even for the blink of an eye, or a flash of lightning, without outside help or support.

If one wants to understand the water element in Mount Meru, Mount Cakkavāḷa, or the Great Earth, one should concentrate only on the characteristic of cohesion, without being distracted by the hardness therein, which is the property of the earth element. Concepts of colour and form are likely to obstruct the meditator's comprehension. This is because knowledge lacks definition, with the result that, as one tries to contemplate the arising and vanishing of phenomena, the mind gets murky. For unless the ultimate truth of a given phenomenon (in this case, the water element) is perfectly comprehended, the reality of impermanence (*anicca*), suffering (*dukkha*), and non-self (*anattā*) will not be understood.

As has been explained in connection with the earth element, here too when one clearly comprehends cohesion as the ultimate truth of the water element, one will realize that no substance, solidity, mass, or form truly exists, even in Mount Meru or in the Great Earth; and that, apart from the cohesion that characterizes all materiality, one's concepts about shape or form or colour, of clouds, the sun, the moon, or trees, for example, are as insubstantial and illusive as the reflected images of shapes and colours in a mirror or on the surface of clear water. When such clear comprehension of cohesion is gained in respect of Mount Meru or the Great Earth, there will be no difficulty in realizing this fact in living beings as well, be they men, *devas,* or *brahmās*. In fact, what is necessary is comprehending this element in living beings. We begin with Mount Meru and the Great Earth simply to emphasize the falsity or deception in concept, form, shape, and colour in the greatest masses of material phenomena, so that it will be more readily seen in respect to lesser materiality, such as living beings.

One should first master the skill of comprehending this element in oneself from head to foot, however, before trying to contemplate it in others.

Here ends the analysis of the element of cohesion.

Analysis of the Fire Element

The element of heat or the fire element (*tejo-dhātu*) has the property of heat or cold. The fire element is, in the ultimate sense, the mere property of heat or cold. Heat or cold is responsible for the growth and sustenance of the three other coexistent elements. Through maintaining an appropriate thermal degree in things, the heat element provides the necessary function of maturing and invigorating the three other elements in any given physical phenomenon. Take eggs, for example; in a nest they need the mother hen's body heat to hatch successfully. The heat they acquired while in the mother's womb is not enough to sustain them. Without the constant warmth of brooding, they simply rot.

In the same way, the fire element is like the mother hen, and the remaining three elements are like the yolk of the egg. Only in combination with the fire element can hardness (the earth element) come into existence. Only in combination with the fire element can cohesion (the water element) take place. Only in combination with the fire element can motion or quivering (the wind element) occur. Without the presence of the fire element, therefore, the three coexisting elements cannot function.

The property of cold (the fire element) is responsible for the existence of all forms of water, including the seas, the great oceans, and the great layer of water that supports this Great Earth. It is this element that sustains them. The fire element is also responsible for the existence of Mount Meru, Mount Cakkavāḷa, and the Great Earth.[4]

When the meditator singles out the fire element as the object of contemplation, he must concentrate only on the coldness in cold objects and the heat in hot objects, without letting in concepts of colour, form, or size. It will then become evident that in neither heat nor cold does there exist the slightest substance, not even a hundred-thousandth part of an atom. When this fact has been clearly comprehended, the meditator understands that what he has all along considered big or grand forms, shapes, and colours, such as the sun, the moon, and clouds, are mere concepts and that they have no more real substance than reflections in a mirror or on the surface of clear water.

In contemplating the fire element in one's body, one should focus on as much of one's body as one's concentration can manage. When the meditator has fully understood the ultimate truth of the fire element in his own body, it will also become clear that everything in the universe, including all living beings, is subject to the same truth.

Here ends the analysis of the heat element.

Analysis of the Wind Element

If we watch a flame, we can see that it is in motion; the same with the accompanying smoke. Just as the fire element is responsible for the combustion, the wind element keeps the combustion in the form of a flame or an active fire. The maintenance of the fire and of its heat and light, the quivering of the flame, the spread of the smoke, and the growth of the fire as things around it catch fire—all are the function of *vāyo-dhātu*, the element of motion, or the wind element.

The wind element has exactly the same function in all materiality. It is due to the presence of the wind element that heat and cold are transmitted throughout any given material object. When we kindle a fire, we start with a tiny piece of fire which we put to the fuel. That little fire catches on to the fuel, assisted by the wind element, which, in fact, is the motive force of the fire element. This motive force spreads the heat of the fire element to all things around the original fire, and, if they are inflammable, they may catch fire. When the motive force is weak, we may assist with some external motive force by using a fan, a bellows, or a blower.

This motive force accompanies both heat and cold. It is important to note carefully that heat is one phenomenon and that the accompanying motive force is another. Of course, it is the same with cold. The property of heat or cold is a distinct property that belongs to the fire element. The motive force is the distinct property belonging to the wind element.

The wind element, due to this motive force, is the vital energy of the three other coexistent elements of earth, water, and fire. The other three are borne by the wind element wherever it carries them. When the force gets very strong, it is called a gale. This force is present in such things as air pillows and air mattresses, where it provides the necessary function of a cushioning effect. This property of the wind element, according to the scriptures, is called support (*vitthambhana*).

In all physical phenomena beginning with Mount Meru, Mount Cakkavāḷa, and the Great Earth itself, the element of cold (*sīta-tejo*), assisted by the motive force of the wind element, arises every moment to sustain the prolonged existence of those physical phenomena until their total disintegration at the destruction of the universe after a world cycle (*kappa*). Contemplate this fact with mindfulness until you grasp it well.

The arising of mind-originated materiality (*cittaja-rūpa*) throughout the body as a result of a certain consciousness (*citta*) that arises at the heart-base (*hadaya-vatthu*), the arising of temperature-originated materiality (*utuja-rūpa*), the dissemination of nutriment throughout the body when food is taken, the gradual growth and development of the embryo from its ultra-microscopic liquid form (*kalala*) to a full-size living being, and the germination and growth of all vegetation—all these phenomena arise due to the motive force of the wind element. Try to visualize this fact with your mind's eye, when you contemplate the phenomenon of the wind element in all things, animate or inanimate, beginning with Mount Meru, Mount Cakkavāḷa, and the Great Earth, until the mere property of motion becomes clear. You must then contemplate the same truth in your own body from head to foot. The same as in contemplating the other elements, color, form, and shape, formerly accepted as truth by convention, will stand in the way. These are mere concepts (*paññatti*), not real, nonexistent. They must be dispelled by penetrating knowledge (*paṭivedha-ñāṇa*), until you fully realize the ultimate absence of form or substance in these phenomena and they appear as no more than images in a mirror.

Here ends the analysis of the element of motion.

The Interdependent Nature of the Four Great Elements

The four great elements, namely: hardness, cohesion, heat or vital warmth, and motion or motive force, are inherently different from one another. They exist together with hardness as a common base. They arise together, stand (momentarily) together, and vanish together. When hardness fails, the three other coexisting elements lose their base and vanish. When cohesion fails and the binding force disappears, the three other elements disintegrate. When heat or cold fails, i.e., the vital warmth goes out and the function of sustaining life stops, the remaining three elements lose their vital force and die out. When the distending function of the wind element fails, the remaining three lose support and collapse together.

The fire element can quiver with its inherent heat or cold only when assisted by the wind element. When the motive force of wind fails, the fire element also dies down in no time. Likewise, the hardness of the earth element depends for its stability and support on the wind element; when this support fails, hardness disappears. Also cohesion, the water element, cannot exist without the supporting function of the wind element. In this way, the four great elements, each with its own property, are interdependent. Failure of one spells destruction for all.

Exactly how the four great elements function in all things, animate and inanimate, however, is too complex and too subtle to understand; in fact, it is truly incomprehensible (*acinteyya*). Their inherent powers are also incomprehensible. Mastery of their nature through insight in pursuing the Buddha's teaching of the Noble Eightfold Path leads to wisdom which penetrates Nibbāna (*paṭivedha-ñāṇa*), which is also called supramundane wisdom (*lokuttara-vijjā-ñāṇa*). In the mundane sphere, mastery of these elements entitles one to supernatural powers. A middling knowledge of them enables one to be proficient in science, for example, in medicine, in chemistry, or in engineering.

Of the four great elements, the heat element is supreme. All physical phenomena, animate or inanimate, from the entire universe, the Great Earth, and the water below the earth's surface, down to the tiniest things, depend on heat for their existence.

The full understanding of the powers of the heat element lies within the province of the all-knowing Buddha.

Here ends the exposition of the interdependent nature of the four great elements.

Analysis of the Space Element

The four great elements, earth (*paṭhavī*), water (*āpo*), fire (*tejo*), and wind (*vāyo*), commonly arise together as groups or units of matter due to (*kamma*), mind (*citta*), temperature (*utu*), or nutriment (*āhāra*). Each group or unit of matter consists of all four elements. The element that separates these groups one from another, is called space or voidness (*ākāsa*), or "that by which an object is delimited" (*pariccheda-rūpa*). When the four great elements arise together and perish together, it is only the elements within an individual unit which do so. The neighbouring units, separated by space, are not affected.

To the ordinary eye, mass or form is seen as the preconceived shapes of living beings or external physical objects. The space between the ultra-microscopic material units that make up the form of a living being or an object is not perceived. In all physical phenomena, beginning with Mount Meru, Mount Cakkavāḷa, and the Great Earth, composed of the four great elements, there are spatial interstices between every unit of matter. Thus, between all masses of materiality there is voidness or space, comparable, in principle, to the open sky above the earth. It is very important to gain a clear comprehension of this element of space because it is essential for the understanding of material units, and this in turn is essential for the understanding of the three characteristics of all phenomena. To gain insight into the three characteristics of all phenomena, one needs to contemplate space in all physical objects, animate or inanimate, and to perceive its presence.

The element of space, unlike the four great elements, does not actually arise from any origin. It has no objective reality. It is only a delimiting element that appears whenever material units come into being due to the four causes given above. Since it does not arise and vanish, one does not need to contemplate it in order to gain insight into its impermanence, suffering, or non-self. Knowledge of the three characteristics of phenomena does not come from contemplating space as an object in itself. Rather, the element of space needs to be properly perceived as a necessary condition for the understanding of the three characteristics of the four great elements—earth, water, fire, and wind.

Here ends the analysis of the space element.

Analysis of the Element of Consciousness

The element of consciousness (*viññāṇa-dhātu*) is the element through which one knows sense objects. Consciousness is of six kinds, namely:

(1) Eye-consciousness (*cakkhu-viññāṇa-dhātu*).
(2) Ear-consciousness (*sota-viññāṇa-dhātu*).
(3) Nose-consciousness (*ghāṇa-viññāṇa-dhātu*).
(4) Tongue-consciousness (*jivhā-viññāṇa-dhātu*).
(5) Body-consciousness (*kāya-viññāṇa-dhātu*).
(6) Mind-consciousness (*mano-viññāṇa-dhātu*).

Of these:

1. Eye-consciousness is the consciousness that arises by way of the eye when the eye comes into contact with visible objects.
2. Ear-consciousness is the consciousness that arises by way of the ear when the ear comes into contact with sounds.
3. Nose-consciousness is the consciousness that arises by way of the nose when the nostrils come into contact with smells.
4. Tongue-consciousness is the consciousness that arises by way of the tongue when the tongue comes into contact with tastes.
5. Body-consciousness is the consciousness that arises by way of the body when the body comes into contact with tactile objects. (Put in simple terms, it is the sense of touch.)
6. Mind-consciousness is the consciousness that arises by way of the heart-base (*hadaya-vatthu*) when the heart-base comes into contact with mental objects, either good, such as faith (*saddhā*), morality or virtue (*sīla*), learning (*suta*), and charity or giving (*cāga*), or bad, such as greed (*lobha*), hatred or anger (*dosa*), and delusion (*moha*).

Generally speaking, when the eye sees a visual object, a person thinks, "I see it." This is, in fact, a wrong view, induced by attachment to eye-consciousness. The fact of seeing is merely a distinct phenomenon (without anyone who sees) and needs to be understood clearly through insight.

Likewise, the phenomena of hearing sounds, smelling odors, tasting flavors, and touching tactile objects should be understood clearly through insight.

When the mind thinks thoughts or knows things, a person generally thinks, "I think of this or that" or "I know this or that." This is, in fact, the wrong view of personality view (*sakkāya-diṭṭhi*). The arising of a thought is a distinct phenomenon and needs to be understood clearly through insight.

Let me now explain how this insight comes about.

The physical body may be likened to an open sore, and the six kinds of consciousness to maggots that infest the sore at various points. Since consciousness is a mental phenomenon, you have to imagine it arising, dependent on the six sense-bases (eye, ear, nose, etc.). Let me give you another simile: imagine the six sense-bases as six very clear patches of water, and the six kinds of consciousness as reflections appearing on those individual patches of water.

These two similes help to convey the fact that sense data or sense-objects are distinct from and external to the sense-bases. Although consciousness is imagined as some real thing at first, after extensive contemplation, it will become clear that consciousness is purely a mental state. Even though the mental states are not clearly recognized, and they appear as reflections on patches of clear water, or dew drops falling on a piece of glass, it does not matter. The main purpose is to comprehend the phenomena that are commonly called "seeing," "hearing," "smelling," "tasting," "touching," and "thinking." If the similes—a sore and maggots and patches of water and reflections—do not help dispel the personality view, such that the deluded "I" still persists within the six kinds of consciousness, insight is still far beyond you. Only when your earlier ingrained concept of "I see it, I hear it," etc., disappears and you properly comprehend and firmly grasp the real occurrence of consciousness, can you be sure that you have gained the knowledge of comprehending the Dhamma.

The arising and vanishing of phenomena take place at tremendous speed, much, much faster even than a flash of lightning. According to the *Visuddhimagga* "they arise and vanish like lightning in space." Thus, you have to realize that phenomena arise and vanish extremely rapidly, even within such fleeting moments as the blinking of an eye.

This contemplation of impermanence, suffering, and non-self is the way to break up the persistent concepts of permanence, happiness, and self or ego, with their erroneous belief in a being, a person, or a life. When the ephemeral characteristic of all phenomena, which last not even as long as a flash of lightning, is seen through, the truth that such phenomena are not at all reliable also becomes clear; and when this is thoroughly understood, the suffering and the non-self, non-person, or non-life characteristics of these phenomena will automatically come to light. This understanding is no other than the knowledge of comprehending the Dhamma.

The fleeting nature of phenomena is, therefore, aptly compared in the scriptures to a flash of lightning. However, the rapidity of the occurrence of mental phenomena is far greater than that. Their arising and vanishing may even be reckoned in hundreds of thousands of times within a flash of lightning. The rapidity is beyond human comprehension. Therefore, it is not advisable to make such subtle phenomena the object of one's contemplation. Try as one might, these phenomena will not be comprehended even after contemplating for a hundred or a thousand years. The meditator who tries this will not gain a single ray of insight, but will be beset by more befuddlement and despair. The scriptures say that mental phenomena take place billions and trillions of times within the blink of an eye, a flash of lightning, or the snap of your fingers. Now the duration of the blink of an eye itself is so fleeting that attempting to contemplate the occurrence of mental phenomena to the billionth or trillionth part of that duration becomes sheer folly. Therefore, one should be satisfied with comprehending the unreliable and transient characteristic of all phenomena, which, after all, is the main purpose.

As for the exact nature, i.e., the swiftness, of mental phenomena, the understanding of which is the domain of the wisdom of the All-knowing Buddha, one has to accept the authority of the scriptures. Any talk about contemplating the three characteristics of mental phenomena is mere humbug. It is never based on practice, but only on hearsay from the scriptures. If someone were to try it, it would be a far cry from insight.

Here ends the analysis of the element of consciousness.

A Brief Exposition of the First Light of the Buddha's Teaching

A fair understanding of the six elements—the four great elements together with the element of space and the element of consciousness—that underlie all phenomena, internally within oneself and externally in all things, beginning with Mount Meru, Mount Cakkavāḷa, and the Great Earth, as explained above, constitutes the first light of the Buddha's teaching that establishes one in the Dhamma. Until one is so established, one wallows helplessly in the dark quagmire of stark ignorance of the Dhamma. Therefore, having had the golden opportunity of hearing the Buddha's Teaching, it is appropriate to strive for this light, which is, after all, the only worthy goal for a human being.

Here ends the exposition of the first light of the Buddha's Teaching.

Chapter Three

Detailed Exposition of the Knowledge in Comprehending the Law of Causality

The second light of the Buddha's Teaching is knowledge in comprehending the law of causality (*paccaya-pariggaha-ñāṇa*). What causes material and mental phenomena to arise? What is the origin of these phenomena? What is required to gain this light, this knowledge in comprehending the law of causality?

The Four Causes for the Arising of Materiality

The four great elements, earth (*paṭhavī*), water (*āpo*), heat (*tejo*), and wind (*vāyo*), together with the fifth material element, space (*ākāsa*), are conditioned by four factors, namely, volitional acts (*kamma*), mind (*citta*), temperature (*utu*), and nutriment (*āhāra*). The element of consciousness, as we mentioned above, is conditioned by the six sense-bases (*vatthu*) and their respective sense-objects (*ārammaṇa*). So we have six basic elements, which are conditioned by six basic phenomena (i.e., the four conditions governing materiality *plus* the two conditions governing mentality). A good understanding of these phenomena is required for one to gain this light, knowledge in comprehending the law of causality.

Now the four great elements—earth, water, fire, and wind—arise due to the four conditions mentioned above, but space, however, since it is not conditioned, i.e., "not born" (*jāti*), does not have any arising (*uppāda*). It merely serves to delimit the material units (*rūpa-kalāpa*) conditioned by the four great elements. Hence, one should not look for the origin or cause of space. Therefore, we exclude space from our study of the law of causality.[5]

(1) *Volitional Acts (kamma) as Origin*

Kamma refers to action done in previous existences. This may be, on the one hand, good *kamma*, such as giving, morality (or virtue), etc., or on the other hand, bad *kamma*, such as killing, stealing, etc. The following nine kinds of material phenomena arise due to *kamma*: physical vitality (*jīvita*), heart-base (*hadaya-vatthu*), female sex (*itthibhāva*), male sex (*pumbhāva*), eye-sensitivity (*cakkhu-pasāda*), ear-sensitivity (*sota-pasāda*), nose-sensitivity (*ghāna-pasāda*), tongue-sensitivity (*jivhā-pasāda*), and body-sensitivity (*kāya-pasāda*). All these material phenomena are conditioned by past *kamma*. It is obvious that once physical vitality (*jīvita*) is destroyed in the present existence, no other condition—temperature, nutriment, medicine, or medicinal diet—can restore it. This body dies, that is, the present existence expires, and a new existence arises. It is the same with the heart-base, eye-sensitivity, ear-sensitivity, and all of the material phenomena mentioned above. From their inception, they are all subject to favourable conditions and circumstances for their continued existence throughout the process of their development. Once the process is interrupted, no amount of present efforts can restore them. That is why they are said to be the product or result of past *kamma* only.

The same should be understood with regard to the four great elements born of *kamma*.

Here ends the exposition of volitional acts
as origin of physical phenomena.

(2) *Mind (citta) as Origin*

There are three states of mind (*citta*): (a) wholesome or moral (*kusala*), (b) unwholesome or immoral (*akusala*), and (c) indeterminate or amoral (*abyākata*).

(a) The wholesome state of mind includes giving, morality, love (*mettā*), compassion (*karuṇā*), joy in others' well-being (*muditā*), equanimity (*upekkhā*), confidence (*saddhā*), wisdom (*paññā*), and concentration (*jhāna*).

(b) The unwholesome state of mind includes greed, anger or hatred, delusion, conceit (*māna*), jealousy (*issā*), niggardliness or avarice (*macchariya*), remorse or brooding (*kukkucca*), and ill-will (*vyāpāda*).

(c) The indeterminate or amoral state of mind includes resultant (*vipāka*), kammically non-operative (*kiriya*), rebirth-linking (*paṭisandhi*), passive (*bhavaṅga*), adverting (*āvajjana*), examination (*santīraṇa*), reception (*sampaṭicchana*), registering (*tadārammaṇa*), and deceased (*cuti*).

Mind (*citta*) may also be divided into three kinds of consciousness—in bodily actions, in verbal actions, and in mental actions.

Consciousness in bodily actions varies with the manner of physical movement, such as going, standing, sitting, lying down, bending, stretching, etc. Consciousness in going means the volition that activates the particular deportment. It is this consciousness that brings the foot to make the first step. This is followed by another consciousness which brings the other foot to make another step. Thus, each step is directed by a separate consciousness. As long as this type of consciousness arises successively, steps are made successively. Likewise, in all bodily movements, every little bit of movement is brought about by its own type of consciousness. As an illustration, take a railway engine. Each puff of steam from inside the boiler turns the machinery in a specific stroke, and with each, a puff of smoke escapes from the chimney. Every stroke of the machine, and every puff of smoke from the chimney, is the work of a specific puff of steam. The same principle is observable in other steam engines, such as those in power-generating plants and steam liners.

In the same manner, when you walk, each step that you take is made on account of a particular motivating consciousness, accompanied by its own set of physical phenomena. The consciousness that motivates the first step vanishes at the end of the step when the physical phenomena of that step die away. A fresh consciousness arises for the next step, bringing in a fresh set of physical phenomena. This second step ended, the physical phenomena therein vanish, and the motivating consciousness is no more. In this way if a hundred steps are made, consciousness and an accompanying set of physical phenomena arise and vanish a hundred times. If a thousand steps are made, consciousness and the material states arise and vanish a thousand times. The mentality-materiality pertaining to any step has no effect on the succeeding step. Each perishes the moment the particular step is made. At each step that is made, fresh motions occur throughout the body. All these motions represent fresh arisings of materiality due to fresh arisings of consciousness. Every day we make innumerable bodily movements with every part of our body. The head, the limbs, and all the other parts of the body move in various manners—exhaling, inhaling, blinking of the eyes, moving the lips, etc. This takes place all the time. Each of these has its own consciousness to account for the particular motion. This is how consciousness in bodily actions brings about physical phenomena which are expressed as bodily actions.

Consciousness in verbal actions brings about physical phenomena which are expressed as verbal actions. Whether we speak, shout, laugh, or cry, every minute utterance is the work of a particular consciousness. For instance, when we say: "*Iti pi so bhagavā...,*" each syllable—*I, ti, pi,* etc.—is motivated by its own consciousness. When we say in English: "Homage to the Buddha," each of the words—Homage, to, the, etc.—is motivated by its own consciousness. You must observe this fact carefully. You must also observe that, at the end of each syllable, its motivating consciousness vanishes. This is how consciousness in verbal actions brings about physical phenomena (audible sounds) which are expressed as verbal actions.

Consciousness in mental actions brings about physical phenomena which are expressed as visible aspects of one's mood, generally noticeable in one's eyes, facial expression, and demeanour. Hence, anger can be distinguished from a face that has assumed a reddish aspect under an angry impulse (consciousness). The face likewise assumes distinct expressions under the impulses of kindness, ill-will, goodwill, etc. Observe carefully that there is a consciousness in mental action behind each material phenomenon that finds outward expression.

This, then, is how the four great elements that constitute physical phenomena arise and vanish millions of times each day under the impulses of consciousness that also arise and vanish in a given individual.

Whereas the physical phenomena in walking are conditioned by the consciousness of walking, i.e., the thought-impulses that bring about bodily movement called walking, most people think, "someone walks," "a woman walks," "a man walks," "he walks," "I walk," etc. This persistent view that the walking is necessarily done by some person, i.e., the walker, is the stark Ignorance of Causality.

The truth is that in the bodily movement of walking, the consciousness that motivates it is neither a person nor a being, neither a woman nor a man, neither he nor I, neither human nor *deva.* It is only the element of consciousness (*citta* or *viññāṇa*). The act of walking, caused by the consciousness of walking, is physical phenomena set in motion. Apart from mentality-materiality of walking, there exists no person, no being, no personal entity, no soul, no individual life, no woman, no man, no he, nor I, that walks. In the same way, there is coming, but no one who actually comes; there is standing, but no one who stands; there is sitting, but no one who sits; there is sleeping, but no one who sleeps; there is speaking, but no one who speaks. In any act, there is only the action without anyone who acts. There is no doer, no subject by way of a living entity, nor is there any creator. There is only the arising of physical phenomena which express themselves as going, coming, sitting, sleeping, speaking, etc., under the motivating force or impulse of consciousness, which is the true cause of all such arising. The ability to discern this truth is knowledge in comprehending the law of causality.

Here ends the exposition of mind as origin of physical phenomena.

(3) *Temperature (utu) as Origin*

Temperature that causes the arising of the four great elements, i.e., the physical phenomena, means cold (*sīta-tejo*) and heat (*uṇha-tejo*). Cold causes cold material to arise. Heat causes hot material to arise. In the cold season, cold prevails, making the body cold. In the hot season, heat prevails, making the body warm. In the rainy season, there is a mixture of cold and heat around us, so that at night the body is cold, and during the day it is warm. In the morning, the body is warm; in the afternoon, it is cold. When we stay in the sun, the body gets hot, we feel warm, and there is perspiration. In the shade, the body is cool, we do not feel warm, and it is comfortable. While sleeping or sitting, the body is cool. While standing or walking, it gets warm. When there is exertion, for example, digging, carrying something heavy, or chopping wood, the body gets warm. Then, when the body rests, it gets cool again. Thus, within one day, in every person, innumerable physical phenomena, cold and hot, arise due to temperature, depending on various circumstances. You should carerully observe within yourself the arisings of hot and cold materiality, which occur in turns due to changes in temperature.

This is how the four great elements, which constitute all physical phenomena, arise due to temperature.

One who cannot discern that hot and cold materiality are arising simply due to changes in temperature, is under the stark ignorance of the law of causality. From such ignorance there arises the wrong view that someone who does this or that exists (*kāraka-diṭṭhi*), that is, a firm belief in a doer. There also arises the wrong view that someone who suffers or experiences this or that exists (*vedaka-diṭṭhi*). One who believes in the existence of a doer, may think, "If I wish to enjoy coolness, I can make myself cool." Or "If I wish to make myself warm, I can do so." There is a corollary to this: when one believes that a being begets the result of an action done by a doer, one may think, "As a result of my own efforts to get cool, I am now enjoying the coolness." Or "As a result of my own efforts to get warm, I am now enjoying the warmth."

Further, one may think, "Due to the meritorious deeds done in my previous lives, I am now endowed with high birth, beauty, wealth, etc." Or "Due to unmeritorious deeds done in my previous lives, I am now born an outcast, ugly, disease-ridden, a nonentity, poor, etc." Or "I have to suffer the consequences of what I have done wrong." In all such statements, "I am experiencing this or that thing" indicates belief in the wrong view of the existence of a person, a doer, or a subject of an act. When someone says: "I did the cultivating, so I reap my harvest," the belief in the existence of the person who cultivates is the wrong view of the existence of a doer. When the Light of the Law of Causality is attained, all activities are seen in their true nature, as mere physical occurrences taking place due to changes in temperature. On attaining this knowledge, belief in a doer or a creator or the act of God's creation dissolves.

Here ends the exposition of temperature as origin of physical phenomena.

(4) *Nutriment (āhāra) as Origin*

Nutriment (*āhāra*), which is the fourth origin of the four great elements, i.e., all materiality, refers to food that is taken every day. It is commonly accepted that a person requires at least two square meals a day and that animals, for example, cows, buffaloes, horses, and elephants, also require a certain amount of food. Consider how the lack of food causes certain noticeable physical changes in yourself, as well as in other living beings, and how a timely meal causes other noticeable physical changes. Everyone knows that hunger causes physical weakness and that a full stomach causes a sense of physical well being. Bad food causes sickness, which is manifested in a sick body. Taking medicine or a medicinal diet causes sickness to disappear, which is manifested in a cured or healthy body. In that sickness and health due to food and medicine are related to temperature, we can see the interrelatedness of nutriment and temperature.

Even though it is obvious that the lack of food causes the body to become weak, feeble, tired, and listless, and that the taking of proper food at the right time satisfies hunger and causes the body to become strong, full of vitality, able, and fit, most people, being grossly ignorant of the truth, are deluded into thinking in terms of a *self*. They think, "*I* ate, so *I* am full and *I* feel strong, vigorous, and fine; *my* hunger is satisfied."

When this delusion of a personal identity, with *I* in the centre of everything, is discarded as being false, and when the truth of the origination of physical phenomena due to nutriment causes weak or disabled physical phenomena (i.e., due to a lack of nutriment), and a supply of nutriment causes strong and able physical phenomena, is comprehended, we can say that the meditator has the correct view of the four great elements that make up all materiality. This is knowledge in comprehending the law of causality.

Here ends the exposition of nutriment as origin of physical phenomena.

The Element of Consciousness

Consciousness (*viññāṇa*) arises on account of the dual condition of base (*vatthu*) and its relevant object (*ārammaṇa*). The six sense-bases (*vatthu*) are:

1. Eye-sensitivity, which is the physical base of the faculty of sight (*cakkhu-vatthu*).
2. Ear-sensitivity, which is the physical base of the faculty of hearing (*sota-vatthu*).
3. Nose-sensitivity, which is the physical base of the faculty of smelling (*ghāṇa-vatthu*).
4. Tongue-sensitivity, which is the physical base of the faculty of tasting (*jivhā-vatthu*).
5. Body-sensitivity, which is the physical base of the faculty of bodily sensation or touch (*kāya-vatthu*).

6. The heart-base (*hadaya-vatthu*), which is the physical base of mind.

The six sense-objects are:

1. Visual objects (*rūpārammaṇa*) or colour (*vaṇṇārammaṇa*) for the eye-sensitivity.
2. Sounds (*saddārammaṇa*) for the ear-sensitivity.
3. Odors (*gandhārammaṇa*) for the nose-sensitivity.
4. Tastes (*rasārammaṇa*) for the tongue-sensitivity.
5. Tactile objects (*phoṭṭhabbārammaṇa*)—such as heat or cold, soft or rough, etc.—for the body-sensitivity.
6. Thoughts or infinitely varied mental phenomena (*dhammārammaṇa*), for the heart-base.

How Consciousness Arises

Consciousness is conditioned by the respective sensitivity and its object in the following ways:

1. Eye-consciousness (*cakkhu-viññaṇa*) arises when eye-sensitivity (*cakkhu-vatthu*) comes into contact with a visual object (*rūpārammaṇa*).
2. Ear-consciousness (*sota-viññaṇa*) arises ear sensitivity (*cakkhu-vatthu*) comes into contact with a sound (*sotārammaṇa*).
3. Nose-consciousness (*ghāṇa-viññāṇa*) arises when nose sensitivity (*ghāṇa-vatthu*) comes into contact with an odor (*ghāṇārammaṇa*).
4. Tongue-consciousness (*jivhā-viññāṇa*) arises when tongue sensitivity (*jivhā-vatthu*) comes into contact with a taste (*rasārammaṇa*).
5. Body-consciousness (*kāya-viññāṇa*) arises when body sensitivity (*kāya-vatthu*) comes into contact with a tactile object (*phoṭṭhabbārammaṇa*).
6. Mind-consciousness (*mano-viññāṇa*) arises when the heart-base (*hadaya-vatthu*), comes into contact with objects of thought (*dhammārammaṇa*).

Let me briefly state here that the mind-consciousness element (*mano–viññāṇa–dhātu*) includes mind-element (*mano–dhātu*), which I will not discuss.

Further Explanation and Examples

When the eye comes into contact with a visual object, the impact produces eye-consciousness, which in common usage is "seeing." We can compare this to the reflection of a face in the mirror. The smooth surface of the mirror may be likened to the eye-base, which is capable of visual sentience. The face reflected in the mirror is like the visual object. When the image of your face falls on the surface of the mirror, it is reflected in the mirror. In the same way, when the eye (we might also say "eye-sensitivity") comes into contact with some visual object, eye-consciousness arises. When your face turns away from the mirror, the reflection of your face in the mirror disappears. You do not see it. Similarly, when the eye turns away from the visual object, eye-consciousness disappears. There is no "seeing." If you turn it toward the object again, eye-consciousness arises again, and, if you turn it away again, eye-consciousness disappears again.

Eye-consciousness (or seeing) is a phenomenon that can arise only while the eye is in contact with the object. When there is no contact, no eye-consciousness can arise, in which case, you do not see the object. Thus, what is called "seeing" is only the function of eye-consciousness, which arises, in the natural state of things (*dhammatā*), due to contact between the eye and the visual object. If there is no eye (eye-sensitivity), there can be no eye-consciousness. Likewise, if there is no visual object within the range of the eye-sensitivity, again there can be no consciousness; there is nothing to see. It is important to note that eye-consciousness is a temporary phenomenon, only a momentary occurrence (*āgantuka-dhātu*), continually arising and vanishing, occasioned by contact between the eye and a visual object.

This analysis can easily be understood in exactly the same way in regard to ear-consciousness, nose-consciousness, and tongue-consciousness.

The arising of body-consciousness takes place throughout the body from head to foot, externally as well as internally, whenever the body (body-sensitivity) comes into contact with a tactile object. Body-sensitivity seems more complex than the other physical senses because it may be only on the skin or it may be deep inside the body. It also includes all sorts of aches, cramps, and itches, as well as feelings of hot and cold.

The simile of the mirror image can be applied to all of these five kinds of consciousness, the same as with the arising of eye-consciousness.

The arising of mind-consciousness takes place due to contact between the heart-base and:

1. Past mental objects, such as:
    (a) past efficient (potent) action (*kamma*).
    (b) a symbol (sign) of that past action (*kamma-nimitta*).
    (c) a sign of the tendencies for further rebirth (*gati-nimitta*).

2. Present mental objects, wholesome and unwholesome. Consequently, mind-consciousness may be in a:
    (a) passive state (*bhavaga-citta*), sometimes called life continuum, which is not active thinking.
    (b) unwholesome state (*akusala-citta*), such as greed, hatred, delusion, ill-will, or covetousness.
    (c) wholesome state (*kusala-citta*), such as faith or knowledge.
    (d) random or idle thoughts (*vitakka*).[6]

All arisings of the six kinds of consciousness must be understood according to the simile of the mirror image.

The inability to comprehend the truth that the six kinds of consciousness arise each due to momentary contacts between the sense-organs or sense-bases and their respective objects—which are commonly spoken of as seeing, hearing, smelling, tasting, touching and thinking, and which are actually separate and distinctive phenomena covering the whole set of the five aggregates—is the stark ignorance of the dhamma, the first stark ignorance.

The lack of understanding of the origin of the six kinds of consciousness, that they arise on the dual cause of sense-base and sense-object, is the stark ignorance of causality, the second stark ignorance. From this ignorance arises the wrong view of a doer or a creator. This view firmly holds that for all actions, there exists a doer, a creator. In other words, all existence means persons and their doings. A personal entity such as "I" or "he" or "she," etc., is responsible for seeing, hearing, etc. We are taught as children that "*I* see with *my* eye and *I* hear with *my* ears, and we take this literally when we become adults. This belief is the only truth an ignorant person holds: he rejects any other cause. All such views that tenaciously hold to the idea of a doer or a creator are wrong.

The wrong view that there is an agent or doer, the view that all the perceptions—seeing, hearing, tasting, smelling, touching, thinking—are actions done by someone and that without some person who sees and hears, etc., they can't take place, is called *kāraka-diṭṭhi*. This view does not accept that these perceptions arise simply through the dual cause of sense-bases and sense-objects, and tenaciously holds onto the idea of a doer or a creator.

An ignorant one holds firmly to this belief, rejecting any other cause. He does not understand that all phenomena arise due to the four conditions—*kamma*, mind, temperature, nutriment—and the dual phenomena of sense-base and object.

Such a person may think, "Due to meritorious deeds done in my previous lives, I am now endowed with high birth, beauty, and wealth," or "Due to unmeritorious deeds done in my previous lives, I am now born an outcast, ugly, disease-ridden, a non-entity, and poor. I must suffer the consequences of the misdeeds I have committed." This is the wrong view that there is one who experiences (*vedaka-diṭṭhi*). Both views, that of a person who does and that of a person who suffers the action of another, are wrong and constitute the stark ignorance of the law of causality. When the light, knowledge in comprehending the law of causality, is attained, all these activities are seen in their true nature, as mere physical phenomena taking place due to the conditions we have explained. On attaining this knowledge, all belief in a doer, one who suffers, a creator, or any act of God's creation, dissolves.

One who comprehends the phenomena of the six kinds of consciousness that arise due to the dual cause of sense-organs or sense-bases and their respective objects—seeing, hearing, smelling, tasting, touching, knowing, or thinking—attains the knowledge of causality, the second great light. This light dispels once and for all the stark ignorance of causality and the wrong view of a doer or creator as the cause of life. Where one clings to the belief that it is due to God that "I see and I hear," etc. occur, not knowing or not accepting the phenomena of the dual cause of the six kinds of consciousness, one also errs in the wrong view of a doer or creator. It should be noted the same ignorance lies at the root of the creator concept too.

End of detailed explanation of the knowledge in comprehending the law of causality.

CHAPTER FOUR

A Detailed Explanation of the Knowledge in Realizing the Three Characteristics

What is the minimum understanding of the three characteristics needed to gain the knowledge in realizing the three characteristics (*lakkhaṇa-paṭivedha-ñāṇa*)? What are the fundamental phenomena that need to be understood?

One must understand the inherent nature of the three characteristics in the six basic elements: *paṭhavī-dhātu, āpo-dhātu, tejo-dhātu, vāyo-dhātu, ākāsa-dhātu,* and *viññāṇa-dhātu.*

Of the five material elements (*viññāṇa* being a mental element), *paṭhavī-dhātu* is the key, for it is the very basis of all materiality. It is on this element that the Great Earth, with the great oceans, mountains, countries, structures, and human settlements is founded. If one can comprehend the impermanence of the Great Earth and can visualize in one's mind its crumbling, disintegration, and vanishing, one will without further effort see the ephemeral nature of all the countries, cities, and human settlements. Similarly, when one has fully realized that instability, ephemerality, and a constant state of decay are the ultimate characteristic of *paṭhavī* as the basis of all materiality, one can without further effort extend the knowledge to include the remaining elements of water, wind, and fire, constituting all material phenomena.

The Three Characteristics

Now, I shall deal with the three characteristics. The characteristic of impermanence (*anicca-lakkhaṇa*) means that a thing is momentary, vanishing as soon as it has risen. It is called *anicca* because it has the nature of destruction and decay ("*khayaṭṭhena aniccaṃ*").

The characteristic of suffering (*dukkha-lakkhaṇa*) is the danger that lurks in the alluring attractions of material things. Just as a leper in advanced stages does not dare to partake of rich delicious food, but must decline any that is offered, so also the wise are not attracted to material things. For the apparent greatness and pleasures of human or celestial existence are all fraught with the inherent danger of defilements, which keep one in the recurring process of aging, decay, and death. It is called *dukkha* because of its nature of danger and dreadfulness (*bhayaṭṭhena dukkhaṃ*).

The characteristic of insubstantiality (*anatta-lakkhaṇa*) is the absence of substance in materiality. No substance that can be called the "essence" of a person exists. As we have seen in our discussion of the previous knowledges, the ultimate truth of materiality-mentality disproves the existence of a person—just as all basic structural materials are only timber or bamboo and not house, monastery, temple, rest-house, or pandal. It is called *anattā* because it lacks substance or essence ("*asārakaṭṭhena anattā*").

The characteristic of *dukkha*, suffering or ill, is fully realized only when one attains *arahatta magga*, the fourth and final stage of the Path. The other two can be realized at earlier or lower stages. Of these two, however, the worldling must first grapple with the characteristic of non-self (*anatta-lakkhaṇa*), which includes the deluded and erroneous personality view, the view of a real self. For this he must necessarily comprehend the characteristic of non-self in all compounded things, which is, in fact, implicit in the characteristic of impermanence.

> "For one who perceives impermanence, O Meghiya, the peception of non-self is established." ("*Aniccasaññino Meghiya, anattasaññā saṇṭhāti*") (Udāna 4.1)

Therefore, I will now clearly explain the characteristic of impermanence with a view to throwing light on the characteristic of non-self.

Examining the Fire Element

In discussing the knowledge of comprehending the Dhamma, we met the six basic elements of materiality. We shall now begin by examining *tejo-dhātu*, the element of heat or the fire element and its characteristics of impermanence and non-self (no-essence). *Tejo* comprises heat and cold, which are known by the world as such, but which are primary elements that belong to *tejo*. Now heat and cold are of opposite nature, each being the antithesis of the other. When cold prevails, heat is absent, and vice versa. What the world calls a being or a person is born only once and dies only once. There are no repeated arisings of a person during his lifetime, nor repeated vanishings or cessations. *Tejo*, as a basic element in the body of all living things, arises quite a number of times in a day, and vanishes in as many times. During the course of any single day, we might say: "Oh, now it is no longer warm; it is getting cold" or "It is no longer cold; it is getting warm now." That being so, *tejo* arises and vanishes in its own way, whereas what is believed to be a person, an individual, does not have the same arisings and vanishings. No identity exists between *tejo* and the assumed personal entity of a being. Thus, in the Abhidhamma sense it is erroneous to speak of "someone" feeling warm or cold when *tejo* becomes hot or cold. It gets warm or cold as a mere phenomenon of *tejo*; no one is feeling warm or cold in the ultimate sense. For, apart from that phenomenon, there is no person, no personal entity.

Since the so-called person or being does not, in the ultimate sense, correspond to *tejo*, a basic element with its own characteristic, it is evident that heat and cold are void of a self (*anattā*). Neither of them connotes a person or a being. If it were so, then the same phenomenon of arisings and vanishings should hold true both of *tejo* and the so-called person. If *tejo* were a person, then, like the so-called person, it should also decease only once in a person's lifetime. As a matter of fact, *tejo* arises and vanishes many times a day, and turns from hot to cold every now and then. These changes are very noticeable. We know when it is hot, and we know when the heat vanishes. We also know when it is cold, and we know when the cold vanishes. If this phenomenon of hot and cold were indeed a person, then we would consider that the person arises and vanishes every time heat or cold arises and vanishes. That, however, is not the case. Though we notice that heat and cold arise and vanish many times a day, we generally do not consider that a person arises and vanishes in as many times a day. We hold the view that a person, once born, dies only once in his lifetime. Thus, the incongruity is plain enough. Heat and cold cannot be the same thing as a person. Heat and cold do not belong to a person; they cannot be called the substance of a person. They are not a person, not a self. They are merely the element of *tejo*.

This is the impermanent and the non-self character of *tejo*.

The fact of the numerous vanishings, even in the course of a day, is the character of impermanence (*anicca lakkhaṇa*). Since material phenomena have the inherent character of constant decay and vanishing, they are not anything substantial that can be called a person or a being. They are vain things that do not really exist. Hence, they have the character of voidness, non-self (*anatta-lakkhaṇa*).

By saying that there is no substance, we mean that if the phenomenon of heat or cold be taken as a person, then one is assuming that the phenomenon is a substance. In that case, one believes that heat or cold represents a personal entity. In other words, one believes in the existence of a self (*attā*). Now, if heat or cold were a person that has a "self," then either of them should remain unchanged until his death. The fact is, however, that heat and cold change every moment, regardless of the so-called person, who has no control over them. Since that "person" cannot rely on heat or cold as his own self, it is evident that heat and cold have no self (*anattā*).

Certain beings live a hundred years. The heat-and-cold in such a person does not remain constant throughout the hundred years of his life. It does not remain so even for ninety years, nor for eighty years, nor for seventy years—for ten years, for five years, for four years, nor for one year. Therefore, it is clear that *tejo* is not his own self; it is not a self at all. I am repeating myself, but this is a very subtle matter that must be grasped. Bear this point with your entire mind and strive to gain insight.

End of discussion on tejo-dhātu.

The Origination and Character of the Four Great Elements in Combination

The four great elements of earth, water, wind, and fire have been compared to reflections that appear in a mirror. They may be likened to a rainbow appearing while sunlight is passing through a vapoury sky. The emphasis is on their ephemeral character. They arise due to the four main causes—*kamma*, mind, temperature, and nutriment—and vanish due to the same causes. If that transient nature of all materiality has been grasped, when one contemplates one's body the same phenomena will be observed. Not the blink of an eye passes without fresh materiality arising many times, only to decay and disappear as soon as it has arisen. Those arisings and vanishings take place not unlike the frothing, turbulent, steamy water in a big boiler, where the froth forms and disappears in no time. Just as a confused succession of bubbles takes form and dies, the arisings and vanishings of the four great elements in the body will be discerned, all caused and conditioned by the four main factors of *kamma*, mind, temperature, and nutriment, of which the role of nutriment is most vivid.

Conditioned by *kamma*, mind, temperature and nutriment, there arise in the body the element of hardness (*paṭhavī* or earth element), the element of cohesion (*āpo* or water element), the element of life-sustaining heat (*tejo* or fire element), and the element of motion and support (*vāyo* or wind element). None of these four elements possesses any substance, not even so much as an atom. All are mere properties or functions. Therefore, when any one of them decays, all of them are destroyed at once. If the element of fire goes out, the qualities of hardness, cohesion, and motion also die out instantaneously. They cannot survive even for the blink of an eye. If the earth element fails, all the other elements lose their basis. Thus, the qualities of cohesion, heat or cold, and motion or distension, all disappear. Watch closely this happening in your own body.

The rate at which the decaying materiality is instantly and continuously replaced by a successive arising of fresh matter is so rapid that tens of thousands of changes take place within the blink of an eye or a flash of lightning. The rapidity is not visible to the physical eye. The arisings and vanishings going on in a state of flux can only be discerned through insight, contemplating their ultimate nature as explained above. In this state of flux, seen with mental perception, every movement represents the change taking place between the old and the new. To the physical eye, an apparently permanent object is seen as making no movements. If one is not wiser than what the eye can see, one is still a far cry from the ultimate truth—a point that needs to be taken to heart.

When the four main causes that bring about the arising of the properties of hardness (earth-element), cohesion (water-element) and support (wind-element), undergo a change, the coexistent fire-element also fails, which brings about the instant cessation of all materiality making up a given unit of materiality. How this comes about will now be explained.

Fire, as we know from everyday experience, arises dependent on some other matter and consumes that matter. That is the very nature of fire. In the same way, the fire element, as an ultimate fact of materiality, arises dependent on the three other elements of hardness, cohesion, and support; and consumes them all in no time. Fire that burns on garbage instantly burns it into ashes. Fire that burns on oil burns up its fuel-oil. In the same way, fire that burns on kerosene consumes the kerosene. Whatever fuel the fire happens to be fed on is devoured at once. Much in the same way, the element of fire that burns throughout the body in all beings devours the coexistent elements, and this process takes place all the time very rapidly without pause. The devouring of nutriment is much more voracious. That being the case, no materiality, be it the element of earth or the element of water, can last even as long as the blink of an eye or a flash of lightning. Within such short moments they all vanish forever, hundreds and thousands of times. Every such decaying materiality is instantly replaced so that the growth and development of childhood into adulthood is made possible.

In the quest for truth, you have to try to visualize with your mental faculty the incessant phenomena of decay throughout your body. If you can visualize the state of flux quite vividly in yourself, you will perceive vividly how the whole body is made up of new arisings or origination of materiality, as well as of the constant decay. Thus, you will see the truth of the impermanence of all things.

A lamp with a fuel-can containing one litre of kerosene burns up whole litre before it dies out. So long as someone refills the can before it is empty, the level of fuel may not seem to decrease and the flame may not appear to diminish in intensity. Yet, the fact is that both the fuel and the flame feeding on it are dying out every moment. If it were otherwise, there would be no need to replenish the oil. Suppose that the lamp is kept alight the whole night and that fifty litres of kerosene oil have been used up. This amount is evidently what has been consumed by the fire. The fact of the flame consuming its fuel is noticeable to the keen observer. The passing moments of the flame getting weaker, as the fuel gets low before it is replenished, is also observable. Furthermore, everyone knows that to keep the lamp alight the whole night requires a considerable amount of kerosene.

The same holds true with living things. It is the regular meals that supply the fuel for the body. A meal provides the necessary fuel to keep the body whole for a certain number of hours, after which the pinch of hunger comes to be felt. After some time, the body cannot function, as it is not supplied with the necessary food. As the body decays so fast, the fresh arising of materiality, replacing the old, is equally fast. This rapid process, by which fresh matter is needed to replace the worn-out and deceased matter, forces living beings constantly to search for food. That is why the task of keeping this mind and body process going is a compulsive action that is not only demanding, but often exacting.

Imagine the amount of food—cereals, grains, and other crops—produced in this part of the world in the course of one year, and apportion it into monthly quotas for consumption by the population; and then break it down into daily requirements. Think of the magnitude of the daily food consumption. It represents the scale of material replenishment that must be met every day. This enormity of the daily food intake required to keep ourselves alive, so that the material phenomena inside us are kept regularly replenished, indicates the enormous rate of decay that is always overtaking us.

Think of the law of "big fish eat little fish," all reflecting the fundamental fact of keeping oneself fed so as to live. Think of the human drudgery, day in and day out, required to earn one's livelihood amidst all sorts of struggles: the sweating away at one's job, the planning and scheming, the travel and expeditions, the arguments and hagglings, the disputes and fights, the security and precautions, the frettings and fumings, the stress and strain, the cares and woes—all these just for the sake of preserving one's precious little life. If one can contemplate all these, down to their root-cause, one will recognise the dire necessity of sustaining the body by providing fresh fuel. One will see the compulsiveness of keeping oneself alive through nutriment. When one is able to understand this compulsive nature of staying alive through fresh fuel, then the *rate* of consumption of what has been fed into the body will be appreciated. Then the ephemeral character of the body will be seen; the utter helplessness will be seen; the sheer absence of self will be seen.

In short, all the cares that beset living things in the world are due to the rapidity with which all material phenomena arise and decay in the body, big or small. This is the natural order of things in their origination—the characteristic of impermanence and non-self in the natural state of things—which needs to be comprehended.

Attachment to one's body is usually strong. Everybody would like to live a hundred years, or even a thousand years (if possible). This entails sustaining the ever-decaying body by means of fresh fuel so that fresh materiality is caused to arise to take the place of decayed matter. If one comprehends the arising of fresh materiality, due to the fresh feedings in the natural state of the body, and realises its transience and non-self character, lacking reality or substance even in the natural form, then it will not be too difficult to comprehend the altered condition (*vikati*) of the arising of materiality, the transience in the altered state of things, the dissolution (*bhijjana*), the diminution (*khaya*), the destruction (*vaya*), and the emptiness or insubstantiality (*asāra*) of the altered state of things.

By altered conditions that arise (*vikati-jāti*) is meant the occurrence of ailments and diseases, dangers, enemies, suffering from violence (*daṇḍa*), and accidents or misfortunes (*upaddava*).

One should observe that the materiality that composes the body is subject to the ravages of all those dangers and mishaps, and that it is decaying and dying out incessantly. This is called "impermanence due to extraneous causes" (*vikati-anicca*). The nature of insubstantiality due to extraneous causes (*vikati-anattā*) should be seen in the same way. The fresh arisings occur incessantly; there is no lapse between the decayed matter and fresh matter; the process is continuous every moment. Therefore, it is possible for desirable materiality and undesirable materiality to arise in turns at any moment, throughout the whole body. And since the deterioration and decay is also occurring very swiftly, it is also possible that being well suddenly turns to being unwell, pleasantness to unpleasantness. In fact, there is never a moment when such a turn from good to bad cannot occur, for every moment is filled with arisings and vanishings. All fresh arisings are, in the ultimate sense, fresh births (*jāti*). For instance, when we say that we have a sore eye or an ear-ache, this is the arising or birth of some unpleasant feeling.

The disappearance is called impermanence (*anicca*), for what has arisen does not last even a moment, but deteriorates, decays, and dies out. In common usage, we say, "The cold is no more, it is gone." These are but instances of impermanence. By non-self (*anatta*) is meant the insubstantial character of all things, the fact that things actually exist only in a state of flux. In common parlance, we hear such expressions as: "Pleasure does not last, it is only *momentary*"; or "The cold lasts *just a while*"; or "Beauty is *not lasting*"; or "The stiffness *is gone now.*" All these expressions denote the transient nature of all compounded things.

In this body, countless factors are ever present to bring to extinction all good or bad, i.e., desirable or undesirable states, and these factors are both intrinsic as well as extrinsic. The Buddha calls *paṭhavī* (earth element) a poison-mouthed (*kaṭṭha-mukha*) snake. When the snake bites the tip of a toe, the poison instantly reaches the head, knocking the victim unconscious. All at once, the whole body undergoes a tremendous change from the normal condition to a searing physical condition. Not a trace of the normal healthy physical condition is left. The whole body is suddenly filled with frightfully hot physical phenomena. This may be likened to a big bomb filled with fifty litres of high explosive, which, when exposed to a tiny fire through its firing point, turns the entire contents of explosive into a powerful mass of fire.

An instant before, the physical condition of the victim, beginning from the soles of his feet, was in a good or desirable state; it was normal. This is quite evident. The burning heat, the pain, the aching, the stabbing sensation, the cramp, the spasm, the convulsion, the numbness and stiffness caused by snake venom, is a later occurrence bringing severe discomfort and distress. This, too, is evident. If the victim were asked, he or she would say that this pain was caused from something outside and was not there before. However, this knowledge is crude, superficial. Because people do not understand the arising of fresh physical phenomena, they do not know that the earlier healthy physical condition, the old materiality, has decayed. They are quite ignorant of the impermanent nature of material phenomena.

Any fresh feeling or sensation that is noticed in one's body, any arising of pain or disease, means fresh origination of physical phenomena, fresh elements, fresh units of materiality, fresh *facts,* in the ultimate sense. Furthermore, all such fresh origination takes place only to replace the old elements, the old units of materiality, the old facts, which have faded away into nothingness. All this instability and cessation should be properly understood as the characteristic of impermanence.

When one feels a hot sensation arise in any part of the body, or throughout the whole body, it is fresh materiality that has taken birth. Wherever fresh arising occurs, one should realize that previous matter has decayed. When the whole body has perceptibly turned hot, one has to understand that the previous materiality, elements, and units of physical phenomena, have decayed and vanished. The rate of change from old to new, however, is too swift to be noticeable.

Sometimes we feel cold; sometimes we feel some pain, ache, numbness, stiffness, and sprain; sometimes there is itching or irritation—all sorts of unpleasant sensations are felt in our body, now here, now there. Wherever such sensations occur, one should perceive that this occurrence signifies dissolution of old materiality, making it possible for fresh materiality to arise.

It is on account of these extraneous causes of the arising of physical phenomena and their transience, which are liable to befall one at any moment, that one is never free from worry. Even in the midst of enjoyment of life, there looms this prospect of external causes leading to an abrupt change into undesirable states. The range of mishaps is infinite; people live in constant worry about disease, accidents, enemies, etc., and have to be always on guard against them, never enjoying a really carefree moment. Fences, alarm-signals, watchdogs, sentries, and volunteer defence corps are symbols of a sense of insecurity. Even so, people are often obliged to sleep in a hidden spot and to travel incognito so as to fool the would-be enemy. When one contemplates these cares and worries attending us all the time, one can appreciate how burdensome this body is, what a great liability, what suffering (*dukkha*).

This is an explanation showing the sudden and swift change and corruption of the earth element, which is the basis of the physical body as illustrated by the Buddha by the poison-mouthed snake, using the analogy of a snakebite victim and a bomb.

What has been said about the earth element should, by implication, also be noted as applying to the elements of water, fire, and wind, the coexistent elements in any unit of materiality.

Practical Method to Comprehend the Three Characteristics in the Four Great Elements

I shall expand this statement now. Imagine a hard block of lac, wax, or tallow, as big as a man. Expose it to fire thoroughly inside and out. Try to visualize the lump melting away—how the hardness gives way to softness, from moment to moment. Then imagine the fire being withdrawn from the lump, and try to visualize the reverse process—how the softness gives way to hardness, from moment to moment. The yielding of hardness, stage by stage, until there is no hardness left is, in Abhidhamma terms, the deterioration, disintegration and dissolution, or decease of the earth element (*paṭhavī*). The same phenomenon has been referred to in various terms in the Suttanta and the Abhidhamma teachings as cessation (*nirodha*), dissolution (*bhaṅga*), diminution (*khaya*), destruction (*vaya*), passing away (*atthagama*), decease (*maraṇa*), and impermanence (*anicca*).

A yogi who practises contemplation for insight must discern the above process of deterioration; when he can do so, he is possessed of knowledge of the three characteristics (*lakkhaṇatthaya-ñāṇa*).

If you have comprehended the earth element as a poison-mouthed (*kaṭṭha-mukha*) snake, then you will also comprehend the water element as a putrid-mouthed (*pūti-mukha*) snake, the fire element as a fiery-mouthed (*aggi-mukha*) snake, and the wind element as a sword-mouthed (*sattha-mukha*) snake. You will understand the impermanent character of these elements and that they are corruptive, decaying, and constantly changing.

As the water element gets stronger, the cohesiveness of materiality gets stronger stage by stage; and, as it gets weaker, the cohesiveness also gets weaker stage by stage until it disintegrates. These changes illustrate that the nature of cessation, dissolution, diminution, destruction, passing away, decease, and impermanence is inherent in *āpo*.

As the fire element gets stronger, the degree of heat gets stronger and the cold diminishes stage-by-stage; and as it gets weaker, heat is replaced by cold and the cold increases stage-by-stage. These changes illustrate that the nature of cessation, dissolution, diminution, destruction, passing away, decease, and impermanence is inherent in *tejo*.

As the wind element gets stronger, the supporting quality and the motive force become stronger stage by stage; as it gets weaker, matter becomes flaccid or lacks movement. These changes illustrate that the nature of cessation, dissolution, diminution, destruction, passing away, decease, and impermanence is inherent in *vāyo*.

When a yogi clearly comprehends these phenomena, he has attained the knowledge in realizing the three characteristics of existence. Only then is he truly possessed of *vipassanā* insight or *vipassanā-ñāṇa*. A superficial awareness that death awaits everyone, that decay is inevitable, that destruction is inevitable, etc., is not sufficient knowledge, for it is not insight. Hence, such commonplace knowledge is not called the knowledge of the three characteristics. This kind of banal knowledge is displayed even by people of other creeds.

What I have described above is the practical method to comprehend the three characteristics in the four great elements constituting our body.

The Three Characteristics in the Six Kinds of Consciousness

Of the six kinds of consciousness, mind-consciousness is the most crucial. It is also fraught with immense possibilities for misunderstanding with grave consequences, dragging one down to the *niraya* abodes of tortuous existences. Thus, I will begin with it.

Mind-Consciousness

Mind-consciousness (*mano-viññāṇa*) is usually misunderstood to be permanent. It is believed to be lying in the heart all the time as a vital force or "life," having a distinct phenomenon all its own with power to prolong itself. Hence the notions "*I* know," "*I* think," "*I* muse," "*I* ponder," etc. All these concepts are grossly mistaken: they are manifestations of the burning personality-belief, the wrong view that can drag one down to the *niraya* world after one's death.

Mind-consciousness has the heart base (*hadaya-vatthu*) as its physical basis. In the heart there is about a cup of blood, which is continuously agitated like a spring due to the digestive heat (*pācaka-tejo*) lying below it and the life-preserving heat (*usmā*) that is diffused throughout the whole body. The materiality known as the heart-base (*hadaya-vatthu*), as millions of units, floats there in the constantly oozing stream of blood. Mind-consciousness arises from that material base in a continuous process of flux. As it arises, it originally has a dazzling luminosity. This radiant quality of mind-consciousness is described by the Buddha in such statements as:

> "O bhikkhus, this mind (consciousness) is shining." (*"Pabhassaram-idaṃ bhikkhave cittaṃ"*) (Anguttara Nikāya 1:5–6)

The lustre of mind-consciousness is, however, not visible with the eyes. It is to be perceived only. One may try to visualize it with benefit, provided such visualization helps one to comprehend clearly the arising and the disappearance of phenomena, since this transience of nature has been compared to a flash of lightning (*"vijjuppādāva ākāse uppajjanti vayanti ca"*). (Niddesa I 43)

For better concentration, try to fix your attention on a particular spot in the heart as the blood oozes out in a rising and falling motion—maybe in the centre, in the front, at the back, on the right side, or on the left side. In fact, such risings and fallings take place in the heart in hundreds of spots, and, wherever a phenomenon arises, it disappears then and there. This is its nature.

Imagine any sensitive bodily organ the same size as the heart—an eyeball, for example—on which many pin pricks are made. Each prick will cause a sensation of pain to arise at that spot, and the painful consciousness and mental aggregates (*nāmakkhandhā*) will disappear at the same spot. In the same manner, you should be able to see vividly in the mind the arisings and vanishings of consciousness and mental aggregates anywhere at the heart-base.

Let us take an illustration: A small bottle is filled with about a half-cup of a very clear red liquid that can swiftly destroy anything coming into contact with it. A microorganism of extremely delicate nature, dazzling white, that is born in the liquid by its own nature, arises now here, now there, and makes as if to move violently; but, even before the movement can take place, it is dissolved in the red liquid and disappears within the blink of an eye. Visualize the continuous appearance of these microorganisms, now here, now there, and their instantaneous disappearance. The arising and vanishing of mind-consciousness is taking place just like that—mere flashes, or, rather, a series of flashes.

The rapidity of the rising and falling is so pronounced that, wherever one focuses the mind on the heart-base, the whole surface of the red blood will be marked by a continuous succession of these risings and fallings, as if in a state of oscillation. The tenacious conventional concept of "*I* know," "*I* think," etc., holding consciousness or mind as one's own self, must now be readily identifiable with this oscillating phenomenon. If, in spite of such visualization, the old deluded belief in a lasting soul or self—"*I* know," "*I* think"—still persists, the knowledge is not real; it is still superficial. Therefore, do not let that diehard belief, which is a passport to the hellish fires of *niraya*, linger in your thoughts.

When you try to understand the changing phenomena of mind-consciousness at the heart-base, give your attention also to what has all along been taken for granted as your thought. Then you will slowly realize that, in reality, none of your thoughts are there.

As taught by the Buddha:

> "If one knows that the body is like foam and the mind a mirage, he escapes the clutches of Death (*maccu*) and attains Nibbāna." (Dhammapada 46)

Herein, the body is compared to foam to show its unstable and ephemeral nature, and the mind to the mirage to show the *delusion* and lack of real substance.

In the hot season, before the rains arrive, natural reservoirs lie as wide stretches of parched land with cracks showing everywhere. In the midday sun, these dry unvegetated stretches, when viewed from a distance, present a shimmering sea not unlike a vast expanse of water. Herds of thousands of thirsty deer, in search of very scarce water, think that the mirage appearing before them is water, and they rush toward it. When they get to the scorched bed of the reservoir, however, the imagined water still seems some distance away. They try to get there, but there is no water. They may turn back and see the same phenomenon in the centre of the reservoir. In that case, they run back to the centre. The water is not there; it again seems to lie yonder, where they again rush. In this way, there is endless delusion and an endless search for water, where, in reality, there is no water at all. All perish in the vain attempt.

This mirage is, in fact, a product of a slight vapour arising from beneath the earth due to direct sunlight and heat. It is an admixture of the vaporous heat and sunlight that makes it appear to be quivering. It cannot be seen at close quarters. It only appears at a distance where the sunlight plays a role with the rising heat. In contemplating mind-consciousness, one has to remember this elusive phenomenon. The mental constituents (*nāmakkhandha*), i.e., *viññāṇa* and the incorporeal factors, arise constantly, being inclined to mental objects, and vanish as swiftly as the vaporous heat, and, just like the mirage, they lack substance.

The arising and the vanishing must be observed carefully. That the arising and vanishing occur in fleeting succession must be clearly comprehended. That is the essence. Then the character of impermanence is grasped.

After one has comprehended the transient nature of the six kinds of consciousness, as explained above, one should contemplate their dependent origination. When the characteristic of impermanence is well comprehended, the characteristic of emptiness, insubstantiality, or the non-self, becomes evident.

On Eye-Consciousness

"On account of visual objects and eye-sensitivity, eye-consciousness arises." (*"Cakkhuṃ ca paṭicca rūpe ca uppajjati cakkhu-viññāṇaṃ."*) (Paṭṭhāna)

Herein "visual objects" is an Abhidhamma expression. It is an abstract term. To demonstrate what it means, one has to resort to the eight essential properties of matter that constitute a certain physical unit. "Visual object called man," "visual object called cow," "visual object called log," "visual object called post," etc. are all Abhidhamma terms. "I see a man," "I see a cow," "I see a log," "I see a post," etc. are of common usage. Even in the Abhidhamma there are certain terms coined in a concrete sense, like *kabaḷiṅkāra āhāra* (lit., a morsel) for material food. Such usage is called "expressions in concrete terms" (*savatthuka-kathā*). When expressed in this way, the meaning becomes clear. Thus, in the Abhidhamma, these common usage terms (*vohāra-kathā*) are interspersed between abstract terms (*paramattha-kathā*), which are valid in the ultimate sense. For instance, in the Dhammasaṅgaṇī, we come across such words as rice (*odana*), malt gruel (*kummāsa*), meal (*sattu*), fish (*maccha*), and meat (*maṃsa*). Material food is compounded of eight essential elements (as in any unit of matter), of which "nutritive essence" (*oja*) is one. The term *kabaḷiṃkāra* is another Abhidhamma term for that particular element.

Since concrete terms are more readily understandable, I shall use them here. By "visual objects" that are seen occasionally, we mean things that happen to come within our sight, things that have been noticed. From your rising in the morning until going to bed at night, things seen may be noted down serially, but the seeing is actually too varied and complex. It is varied because there are just too many things to count. It is complex because in seeing just one thing—say a man—one part (of his body) is seen first, one part second, and so on: It is to cover this infinite range of seeing that "visual objects" are said to be "seen occasionally." The essential point here is, in this seeing or, rather, in the process of seeing, *each* object is a case for the arising and vanishing of *each* eye-consciousness, one following the other in rapid succession.

Let me expand on this statement.

As one comes within the seeing range of a log, for example, the image of the log is at once reflected on the eye-sensitivity. In the ultimate reality of things, the impact of this image falling on the eye-sensitivity is considerable: it has been compared to the striking of a thunder-bolt. Eye-consciousness arises due to this rude shock, i.e., as and when the image falls on the eye-base. The phenomenon may be likened to the sparks coming out as steel strikes flint in a lighter. The image disappears every time the eye blinks, and at each disappearance of the image, eye-consciousness dies out instantly. Needless to say, the image disappears when the eye turns away from the object. When the blink of the eye is completed, if the eye is still fixed on the object, the image strikes again on the eye-sensitivity, causing fresh eye-consciousness to arise. In this way, eye-consciousness arises in a series. One must take careful note of the fresh arising every time. When the eye turns away from the log to a post, the same thing happens: the image of the log disappears, and the eye-consciousness of the log vanishes; the image of the post appears, and the eye-consciousness of the post arises. When the eye turns away from the post to some other object, again the same thing happens.

Thus, it should be understood that the eye-consciousness arises as and when each visual object is noticed; each consciousness is due to each act of noticing the object.

Eye-consciousness can arise only due to the impact of the image falling on eye-sensitivity. Hence, the text states, "*on account of* visual objects." Thus, eye-consciousness in seeing a log is caused by the log; eye-consciousness in seeing a post is caused by the post. In other words, eye-consciousness caused by the log makes you see the log; eye-consciousness caused by the post makes you see the post. Let your understanding be clear about this and about all your acts of seeing.

To take a simile: A certain woman living during a world-period when the human life span is a hundred thousand years is widowed after her first year of marriage. During her marriageable life of fifty-thousand years, she remarries, and each time she does so, her husband dies after only one year. By each husband she begets a child. In this way, she has married fifty-thousand husbands altogether and has begotten as many children. Now, when we wish to refer to these fifty thousand children, we cannot identify them with reference to the mother, so we have to refer to the respective fathers—"as Mr. so and so's child". Eye-sensitivity is like the mother; visual objects (log, post, etc.) are like the fifty-thousand fathers; each eye-consciousness is like one of the fifty thousand offspring. That is why it is said: "Through coincidence of eye and visual object, the offspring of evil desire is begotten."[7]

Therefore, it is quite true to speak of someone seeing the log through the eye-consciousness born of the log; seeing the post through the eye-consciousness born of the post; and so forth with respect to everything he may happen to see during a day from the moment of his rising to his retiring for the night.

Let us take another simile: Holding a big glass block, someone runs along a path flanked on each side by a thousand trees which are about a man's height. As he passes between the rows of trees, their images of the trees fall *in turn* on the glass block. Eye-sensitivity is like the glass block; the trees are like the various visual objects; and the images of the trees falling in turn on the moving glass block are like eye-consciousness. The appearance and disappearance of each specific image of the trees represents the phenomenon of eye-consciousness.

Various sounds giving rise to ear-consciousness, smells to nose-consciousness, tastes to tongue-consciousness, tactile objects, both internal and external, to body-consciousness—all these phenomena should also be understood in the same way as in the analogy of the eye-consciousness.

On Mind-Consciousness

The range of mental objects (objects of the mind, ideas, or thoughts) is infinite. They may be wholesome or moral (*kusala*), unwholesome or immoral (*akusala*), or ineffective or indeterminate (*avyākata*). The range includes eye-consciousness, ear-consciousness, etc. It includes unwholesome mental properties, such as greed, hatred, delusion, and wholesome and indeterminate mental properties, such as faith (*saddhā*), wisdom (*paññā*), mindfulness (*sati*), contact (*phassa*), feeling (*vedanā*), perception (*saññā*), volition (*cetanā*), one-pointedness of mind (*ekaggatā*), physical life (*jīvitindriya*), attention (*manasikāra*), the seven common mental properties (*sabba-citta sādhāraṇa*), initial application (*vitakka*), sustained application (*vicāra*), deciding (*adhimokkha*), effort (*viriya*), pleasurable interest or joy (*pīti*), desire-to-do (*chanda*), and the six particular mental properties (*pakiṇṇaka*). Also included are phenomena such as the four great elements, the six sense bases, life-force (*jīvita*), nutriment (*āhāra*), birth (*jāti*), ageing (*jarā*), and death (*maraṇa*). All of these are called *dhammārammaṇa*. Furthermore, the objects of the five senses cannot be known without the functioning of mind-consciousness (*mano-viññāṇa*).

Mind-consciousness, therefore, receives impressions via the five physical senses in addition to receiving mental objects. In these six ways, the objects of mind-consciousness arise all the time. They belong to the past, the present, and the future. The past experiences, from the time one is born to the present moment, constitute past impressions. All anticipated ideas pertaining to the future, even extending limitlessly into future existences, also work on mind-consciousness. Furthermore, all secondhand knowledge pertaining to the six senses, which one has learnt from others, also comes within the cognition of mind-consciousness.

Mental conceptions rise and fall incessantly in mind-consciousness. Even while asleep, with the mind in its passive state, the "life continuum" (*bhavaṅga*) directs its attention to either past *kamma*, or the sign of one's past *kamma*, or the sign of one's destination (*gati-nimitta*).[8]

Throughout the waking hours, from rising in the morning to retiring for the night and falling asleep, sense-objects make impressions on mind-consciousness, each in its turn, according to circumstances.

Mind-consciousness takes place in a process. The passive state (*bhavaṅga*) of the mind must receive certain sense impulses through one of the six senses before mind-consciousness arises in the process. The impulse having been received, the mind adverts to it. Only then is it recognized—cognition takes place. With cognition, the thought process continues: full knowledge of the object occurs, and consequent thoughts based on that knowledge follow.

There is never a break in the reception of sense-impressions of one sort or the other at the heart-base. In fact, a horde of them is always present at its door, seeking entry. Hence, the registering of these impressions goes on without a break. These objects of the mind appear and disappear instantly, causing a distinct mind-consciousness, which rises and falls at each such occasion. This goes on ceaselessly. Of course, we are using the word "ceaseless" in the worldly sense as understood by the uninformed average person.

As a matter of fact, each kind of consciousness takes place only at its respective sense-base; it does not take place in any other part of the body. That is to say, when eye-consciousness takes place, all the mental phenomena occur at the eye only, nowhere else. Mental phenomena—which consist of the four aggregates of mentality (*nāmakkhandha*), comprising feeling (*vedanā*), perception (*saññā*), mental formations (*saṅkhāra*), and consciousness (*viññāṇa*); mind or mind-consciousness (*citta*); and the fifty-two mental concomitants (*cetasikā*)—rise together and fall together at the eye-base before another kind of consciousness can occur at another sense-base. Hence, when consciousness is occurring at the ear-base, it does not occur anywhere else. The same holds true for all the six sense-bases. When body-consciousness takes place at a certain spot on the body, all the mental phenomena arise and fall at that particular spot only. When mind-consciousness takes place at the heart-base, all mental phenomena arise and fall only at the heart-base and nowhere else. However, since the mental processes take place with astonishing rapidity, we normally think there is a simultaneous consciousness taking place over the whole body. Even while one thinks that one is seeing something, the eye-consciousness is being interrupted by mind-consciousness at the heart-base innumerable times. In the same way, if there is occasion, ear-consciousness or other kinds of consciousness can arise. For instance, one may see a moving car, hear the sound of its engine, smell the fumes from its exhaust, and wonder whose car it is and where it is going. People think that these phenomena are occurring simultaneously, but that is not the case. They are occurring in very rapid succession. The same process, it should be understood, applies to the other five senses.

As regards the active comprehension of mind-consciousness, the same principle holds. Consciousness that conditions bodily action cannot at the same time be the consciousness that conditions verbal action. Consciousness that conditions verbal action cannot at the same time be the consciousness that conditions bodily action. However, the rapidity of consciousness is such that the switching off and on of consciousness between bodily and verbal actions is not normally noticed. Hence, we think that while we are walking, we can also be talking; or that while talking, we can also make bodily movements, see things, and hear sounds. These seemingly simultaneous occurrences are, in fact, distinct occurrences with their own arisings and vanishings, but they occur too swiftly to be noticed. Although this phenomenon of fleeting consciousness (*viññāṇa*) may actually run into millions and millions within the blink of an eye, the practising *yogi* needs only to comprehend that all these occurrences are distinct phases of arising (*udaya*) and vanishing (*vaya*). The insight into flux is what must be developed.

The Purpose of Insight

The purpose of the development of insight (*vipassanā*) is to have first-hand knowledge to dispel the long-cherished delusion of the belief in a nonexistent person or ego, all the time being conscious of *I*, such as "*I* see, *I* hear, *I* smell, *I* taste, *I* touch, *I* think"—the six kinds of deluded sensual perceptions which pave the way to the fires of *niraya*; as well as, "*I* speak, *I* move, *I* go, *I* come" etc.—all symptoms of stark ignorance of the three characteristics of existence. By being mindful of the flux of the mental and physical phenomena constantly occurring within oneself, and by carefully observing those phenomena at the six sense-bases (eye, ear, nose, tongue, body, and heart-base), one becomes fully aware of when and how they arise and vanish. This is what must be aimed at. Once the arisings and vanishings are clearly seen, from moment to moment, all actions—bodily, verbal, and mental—in their infinite variety, are covered.

When such insight has been properly developed, the ephemeral nature of all materiality-mentality comprising the six basic elements—the four great elements of earth, water, wind, and fire, as well as the element of space and the element of consciousness—will be perceived as mere bubbles or foam, impermanent and insubstantial. Their continuous arising and vanishing from moment to moment will be perceived. Thus, the ever-present origination, decay, ageing, and death, the essential transitoriness will be perceived. This perception is the light of knowledge in realizing the three characteristics of existence.

On gaining this light, one attains the path (*magga*) and the fruition of the path (*phala*). And since the path wisdom virtually leads to the realization of Nibbāna, it is for practical purposes called the knowledge in realizing Nibbāna (*nibbāna-paṭivedha-ñāṇa*).

Here ends the exposition of the knowledge in realizing the three characteristics of existence and the knowledge in realizing Nibbāna.

HERE ENDS THE MANUAL OF LIGHT.

The Manual of the Path to Higher Knowledge

Vijjāmagga Dīpanī

Preface to the Manual of the Path to Higher Knowledge

There are nuances of meaning of Pāḷi words according to the context in which they are found. Thus the word *nāma* may mean either a "name" or a "mental phenomenon," and the word *rūpa* may mean either a visual object or a "physical phenomenon." Much havoc was wrought when some Western Pāḷi scholars rendered into English the Pāḷi term *nāma-rūpa* as "name and form"[9] instead of "mind and matter." This grievous error persists in many later translations that are "descendants" of the aforesaid pioneering ones of the nineteenth century. Aside from the nuances of meaning such as those described above, every Pāḷi word used in Buddhism has two characters, i.e., the character shown in relative or conventional truth (*sammutisacca*) and the one shown in absolute truth or ultimate reality (*paramattha-sacca*).

Experienced writers are well aware of the difficulties they are up against, and of the failure of their predecessors to convey Buddhist ideas through the medium of a language that has no exact equivalent for the words required by Buddhist philosophy. This perhaps accounts for the fact that there are scores of translations of famous Buddhist texts such as the *Maṅgala Sutta* and the *Dhammapada* and no two of them are exactly alike in the choice of words, aptness of expression, style, or rhythm.

Now, being alive to these dangers, Dr. Edward Conze, a scholar of Pāḷi, Sanskrit and Tibetan languages, has prefaced his book *Buddhist Texts Through the Ages* (Oxford 1954), with the remark that "the English equivalent adopted here can be considered as a makeshift only." It is, he says, "impossible to find one English term that contains and can convey the whole wealth of meaning of a term like *"moha."* Such difficulties, he admits, "are inherent in any translation."

To minimize such difficulties and to obviate the necessity of referring the reader to a glossary of technical terms provided at the end of the book, or to footnotes at the end of each page with the aid of asterisk marks, I have provided the original Pāḷi terms in italics immediately after its English equivalent. In this work, no Pāḷi term (except Buddha, *Nibbāna,* and *Sāsana*) has been left untranslated and it is hoped that the reader will approve of this method.

Every attempt has been made to render as true a translation as possible. I have paid special attention to the differences in the construction of sentences between English and Burmese, and, as another translator puts it, to the Venerable Sayādaw's penchant for using extremely long sentences. Many of the subheadings and subtitles are not in the original text, neither are the amplified versions such as the eight Attainments (*samāpatti*), the ten stages of Insight knowledge (*vipassanā-ñāṇa*), and the fire of decay (*jarā*) and death (*maraṇa*). They have been introduced here to assist the English reader.

U Pu, Burma

Editor's Foreword to the Manual of the Path to Higher Knowledge

I considered it a great privilege that when I first met U Pu in Rangoon, in 1981–82, at the home of my then host and hostess U Tha Win and Daw Khin Ma Ma, that he so kindly and readily undertook to translate into English Ledi Sayādaw's *Vijjāmagga Dīpanī* (*A Manual of the Path to Higher Knowledge*), after the work was suggested to him.

When I again met U Pu on a return visit to Burma at the end of 1984, he was in a very poor state of health, and it was with very much regret that after my return to England in early 1985 I learnt that he had died sometime towards the end of 1985 or early 1986. Due to his poor state of health prior to his death, I had been unable to consult him on several matters that might have been further clarified.

My sincere thanks, however, are due to the Venerable Sayādaw U Ñāṇika for his helpful suggestions and comments on several of the points concerned that I discussed with him.

U Pu's request that I should attempt to polish and refine the English of his translation, wherever I thought necessary, took much longer than I had originally envisaged. No doubt there is still room for much improvement, but this will now have to await the outcome of a revised edition or perhaps an entirely new edition at some future date.

S. S. Davidson, Southsea, 1996

Namo Tassa Bhagavato Arahato Sammā Sambuddhassa

Veneration to the Exalted One, the Worthy One, the Supremely Enlightened One

Five Kinds of Higher Knowledge

Higher knowledge is of five kinds:

1. Mastery in the Brahmanical lore (*veda-vijjā*)
2. Mastery in the art of incantations and spells (*manta-vijjā*)
3. Mastery in executing various feats of supranormal character (*gandhārī-vijjā*)
4. Mastery in mundane psychic powers (*lokiya-vijjā*)
5. Mastery in supramundane knowledge of the Four Noble Truths (*ariya-vijjā*).

(1) *Mastery in the Brahmanical lore* means being endowed with the knowledge of the four Vedas, namely:

- (a) Knowledge of the sacred Brahmanical songs, devotion, worship, and propitiation (*Sāma-veda*)
- (b) Knowledge of the sacrificial formula (*Yaju-veda*)
- (c) Knowledge of the mystic and occult powers (*Iru-veda*)
- (d) Knowledge of the Code of Magic, marvels and miracles, etc. (*Athabbaṇa-veda*)

(2) *Mastery in the art of incantations and spells* means being endowed with the knowledge of the following arts and sciences:

- (a) Palmistry or chiromancy
- (b) Divining by means of omens and signs
- (c) Predicting events by watching the movement of heavenly bodies
- (d) Charms, incantations and spells
- (e) Medical practice and pharmacology
- (f) Determining nutritional and other values
- (g) All other knowledge and faculties developed in the present-day world

The two higher knowledges, described above, are referred to in the "Knowledge" chapter of the Book of Analysis (*Ñāṇavibhaṅga*) of the Higher Doctrine (*Abhidhamma*).

(3) *Mastery in executing various feats of supranormal character* means being endowed with the following knowledge and powers:

(a) Making riches (*dhana-siddhi*)
(b) Diving into the earth and rising again just as if in water (*paṭhavī-siddhi*)
(c) Walking on water without sinking just as if on earth (*udaka-siddhi*)
(d) Floating through the air cross-legged just as a winged bird (*ākāsa-siddhi*)
(e) Extending life beyond the normal life span (*āyu-siddhi*)
(f) Exercising supranormal powers of will (*cintāmaya-siddhi*)

These higher knowledges (*vijjā*) and powers (*siddhi*) are mentioned in ancient books dealing with sorcerers (*vijjādhara*), who are of the following kinds:

(a) The sorcerer with the higher knowledge of medicine
(b) The sorcerer with the higher knowledge of diagrams and numerology
(c) The sorcerer with the higher knowledge of the metallurgic art of transmuting mercury into the "philosopher's stone" or "elixir"
(d) The sorcerer with the higher knowledge of the metallurgic art of transmuting base iron into gold or other precious metals

These occult powers correspond to the supranormal powers of celestial beings and also to the higher spiritual powers (*abhiññā*). In the Pāḷi text, The Path of Discrimination (*Paṭisambhidāmagga*), the following passage is found:

> Of these ten kinds of psychic power, what is the psychic power called "supranormal powers of will" (*cintāmaya-iddhi*)? By the term "supranormal powers of will" is meant the phenomena which the sorcerer by reciting spells can make manifest in the illimitable space of the sky, such as a troop of war-elephants rumbling past, a troop of mounted cavalry galloping by, a troop of war-charioteers rolling away, and a troop of armed soldiers marching along. The sorcerer can also create and exhibit in the illimitable space of the sky, the massing of a variety of armed troopers or of a whole army. This, indeed, is what is meant by the term "supranormal powers of the will."

This simile in the Pāḷi texts concerning the term, *cintāmaya-iddhi*, applies with equal force to other kinds of psychic powers, such as mastery in the arts of extending life beyond the normal life span (*āyu-siddhi*), floating through the air cross-legged like a bird (*ākāsa-siddhi*), walking on water without sinking just as if on earth (*udaka-siddhi*), diving into the earth and rising again just as if in water (*paṭhavī-siddhi*), and so on.

In modern times, an aspirant to sorcererhood with mastery in supranormal feats (*gandhārī-vijjā*) should infuse himself always with the sublime virtues of the Three Priceless Jewels, namely, (1) the Enlightened One, (2) the Law of Deliverance discovered, realized and proclaimed by him, and (3) the Community of Holy Disciples and those who live in accordance with the Law. They should seek the goodwill and affection of such powerful deities as:

(a) Forest deities
(b) Hill deities
(c) Tree deities (*rukkhattha-devatā*)
(d) Earth deities (*bhūmattha-devatā*)
(e) Mountain deities (*pabbattha-devatā*)
(f) Deities in charge of charms, spells, magical diagrams, and numerology (*vijjā-devatā*)
(g) Deities in charge of medicinal herbs, stones, and gems with healing powers (*osadhi-devatā*)

A sorcerer with mastery of supranormal feats excells even the supranormal faculties of deities arising from the results of their past meritorious deeds (*kamma-vipākajā iddhi*). This is liable to arouse jealousies that may endanger life or the efficacy of medicinal herbs.

(4) *Mastery in mundane psychic powers* means the powers attained by such hermits (*isis, rishis*) as *Sarabhaṅga*, *Sunettha*, and *Araka*, outside the period of a Buddha's Sāsana after a mastery of mental absorptions through the utmost perfection in the practice of the *kasiṇa* concentration exercises. These psychic powers are the following magical powers (*iddhi-vidhā-abhiññā*):

(a) The divine eye (*dibba-cakkhu*)
(b) The divine ear (*dibba-sota*)
(c) Penetration of the minds of others (*cetopariya*)
(d) Remembrance of manifold former existences (*pubbe-nivāsa*)

(e) Knowledge of specific retribution (*yathā-kamm'upaga*)
(f) Knowledge of future events (or prevision) (*anāgata-abhiññā*)

The stories of sorcerers who exercised these psychic powers are made prominent in many Birth Stories (*jātaka*) and Collected Discourses (*nipāta*).

The exercise of these mundane psychic powers (*lokiya-abhiññā-vijjā*) is also associated with the Self-Enlightened Buddhas (*sammā-sambuddha*), the Silent Buddhas (*pacceka-buddha*), and the Noble Disciples (*ariya-sāvaka*). These psychic powers are embraced within the threefold higher knowledge (*te-vijjā*) and also within the eightfold higher knowledge attainable by the Self-Enlightened Buddhas, the Silent Buddhas, and the Noble Disciples:

(a) Insight knowledge (*vipassanā-ñāṇa*)
(b) Knowledge pertaining to supranormal powers of will (*cintāmaya-iddhi*)
(c) Knowledge pertaining to psychic powers (*abhiññā*)
(d) Knowledge pertaining to the divine ear (*dibba-sota*)
(e) Knowledge pertaining to penetration of the minds of others (*ceto-pariya-ñāṇa*)
(f) Knowledge pertaining to remembrance of former existences (*pubbe-nivāsa-ñāṇa*)
(g) Knowledge pertaining to vanishing and reappearing of beings (*dibba-cakkhu*)
(h) Knowledge pertaining to extinction of all taints (*āsa-vakkhaya-ñāṇa*)

(5) *Mastery in supramundane knowledge of the Four Noble Truths* means being endowed with the:

(a) Higher knowledge of the truth of impermanence (*anicca-vijjā*)
(b) Higher knowledge of the truth of suffering (*dukkha-vijjā*)
(c) Higher knowledge of the truth of impersonality and conditionality (*anatta-vijjā*)
(d) Higher knowledge of the truth of the path leading to the extinction of suffering (*magga-vijjā*)
(e) Higher knowledge of fruition of "path-result" (*phala-vijjā*)

They can also be called "higher knowledge of the Four Noble Truths."

This "higher knowledge of the Four Noble Truths" can be attained only during the period of the Buddha's Sāsana. Outside that period, i.e., during the "dark ages," no one among human beings, deities or the celestial beings of the Brahma world, except the Silent Buddhas (*pacceka-buddha*), are able to make a successful attempt at gaining this higher knowledge.

The Auspicious Period of the Sāsana

Gotama Buddha's Sāsana, which has been prophesied to last for five thousand years, is an auspicious period during which a successful attempt can be made to win the higher knowledge of the Noble Ones, i.e., the higher knowledge of the Four Noble Truths (*ariya-vijjā*).

Only a person who has made a successful attempt and won this higher knowledge can be deemed to be one who has had the supreme good fortune to come across and pay homage to a Buddha or one who has had the supreme good luck to have encountered a Buddha's *Sāsana* in the course of eternity.

In the *Itivuttaka* the Buddha declared:

> Monks, even if a monk should take hold of the edge of my outer cloak and should walk close behind me, step-for-step, yet if he is ignorant of the Doctrine of the Four Noble Truths, then he is far from me, and I am far from him. But, monks, if a monk should be staying even a hundred *yojanas* (each *yojana* is about seven miles) away, yet if he comprehends the Doctrine of the Four Noble Truths, then he is near me and I am near him. Why is this? Monks, that monk sees the Doctrine (*Dhamma*), seeing the Doctrine he sees me." (It 92)

From this discourse it may be inferred that one who has not come across nor seen the Enlightened One (*Buddha*), nor the Law (*Dhamma*) discovered and proclaimed by him, cannot be deemed to have come across and seen the Community of Holy Disciples (*Saṅgha*).

Who Can Attain Higher Knowledge?

What type of person can make a successful attempt and win the higher knowledge of the Noble Ones during the period of the present Buddha Sāsana?

The Buddha has declared that a person who is endowed with the following attributes can make a successful attempt and win the higher knowledge of the Noble Ones:

1. Having absolute confidence in the Enlightened One
2. Being strong and healthy in both wind and limb of the body
3. Having a generous and straightforward nature
4. Being endowed with a keen and steadfast energy
5. Being possessed of knowledge with the power of penetration into the process of arising and dissolution of the mental and physical phenomena of the five aggregates (*khandha*)

This declaration is recorded in such scriptures as the *Aṅguttara Nikāya* (AN 5:135) and others.

The discourse explaining the above statement is as follows:

The First Attribute

> *Saddho hoti saddahati tathāgatassa bodhiṃ.*
>
> "One who is endowed with a deep sense of confidence. One who has absolute confidence in the wisdom and omniscience of the Buddha."

Here ends the description of the first attribute.

The Second Attribute

> *Appābādho hoti appātaṅko samavepākiniyā gahaṇiyā samannāgato nātisītāya nāccuṇhāya majjhimāya padhānakkhamāya.*
>
> "One who is free from ailments. One who is free from diseases. One who is endowed with such digestive (gastric) heat that is neither too hot nor too cold, but has the capacity of dissolving uniformly any morsel of food, thus enabling one to practise meditation with zest and vigour either for mental tranquillity or insight."

In the present age of moral and spiritual decline (*vipattikāla*), endowment with this second quality is extremely rare.

The combustion of the digestive (gastric) fire in a normal human being of the present times is just like the combustion of a straw-fire, hay-fire, or dried-leaf fire. These fires leap up into flames with great ferocity as soon as igniting conditions become favourable. They set ablaze all inflammable objects in the neighbourhood in a short space of time. But these fires are evanescent things (having none of the determination of wood or charcoal combustion). When conditions favourable for their dying out arise, such fires die out abruptly and completely. Continuing with the same analogy, the digestive (gastric) fires of people today are prone to flare up abruptly and die out abruptly. They are thus prone to fall sick easily, to get old and infirm easily, or to die easily. People nowadays also have to reckon with the conditions peculiar to the locality in which they have to reside, the food they eat, the water they drink, the rigours of weather or climate they have to brave, and the degree of effort they have to make to protect themselves from those dangers. Because of the malfunctioning of the digestive or gastric fire, the physical body looks gloomy and lacking in energy and due to the gloomy and lethargic state of the physical body, the mental and intellectual faculties become dull and sluggish. The turbulence in quickly igniting and quickly dying out of straw-fires, hay-fires, and dried-leaf fires, as described in the above example, is due to the fact that these inflammable materials are without a core or substance.

In the case of a person who is endowed with a system of well-balanced digestive (gastric) fires, as explained in the canonical texts referred to above, there is no particular need to make a choice between one locality and another, between one kind of food and another, or between one climatic condition or another, be it of water, wind, earth, or any other condition. There can be no turbulence of any strength or weakness of digestive (gastric) fires enough to produce the slightest indisposition or any other kind of illness. And so this element of digestive fire maintains at all times a state of equilibrium in guarding and protecting the physical body, which is thereby always kept bright and alert. In former ages of moral and spiritual ascendancy (*kāla-sampatti*), even animals of the lower world were endowed with such well-balanced digestive (gastric) fires. In the present age of moral and spiritual decadence, however, only men who are exceptionally gifted (*purisa-visesa*) and who are supported by a strong force of good *kamma* from the past are entitled to be endowed with this kind of digestive fire. People of the present age who are not supported in this way by a strong force of good *kamma* from the past cannot hope for such a blessing as this. They can, however, improve their lot by resorting to elixirs, tonics, or medicines of high efficacy.

The following has been declared in *Nettipakaraṇa* (Nett 23):

> *Sakkateva jarāya paṭikammaṃ kātuṃ.*
>
> "It is, indeed, possible to arrest the natural process of ageing and decay of the physical body."

This passage in the Pāḷi text, which suggests the possibility of arresting the natural process of ageing and decay, bears with it the implication that it is also possible to prevent sickness or disease. The great Sub-Commentary to *The Path of Purification* (*Visuddhimagga-mahāṭīkā*) says:

> *Rasāyana bhesajjaṃ pana suciraṃ pi kālaṃ jīvitaṃ pavattetuṃ sakkoti yeva.*
>
> "There is a sovereign remedy for disease called *rasāyana,* which possesses the power and efficacy to prolong life beyond the normal span of only a hundred years to more than five hundred or a thousand years."

The significance of the term *rasāyana* is comprehensively explained as follows:

> *Rasā āyanti vaḍḍhanti etenāti rasāyanaṃ.*

Meaning: "It is called the powerful tonic or 'elixir' because the blood cells and molecules that draw sustenance from it become charged with nutritive values enduring for more than thousands or tens of thousands of days, months, or years and are kept in this developed state in perpetuity." It means, also, that even though a person is supported by a weak force of good *kamma* accumulated in the past, he can still manage to prolong his life to more than a thousand or ten thousand years in an era or age in which the normal life span is a hundred years. This can only be done by means of outstanding ingenuity and relentless effort in order to produce this kind of elixir with which to transform the features of his physical body.

For the purpose of prolonging one's life, one would also have to take a regular dose of the longevity-promoting medicine prescribed by the Exalted Buddha as follows:

Abhivādanasīlissa
niccaṃ vaḍḍhāpacāyino
cattāro dhammā vaḍḍhanti
āyu vaṇṇo sukhaṃ balaṃ.

To him who habitually pays homage and respect
to those who are his superiors in age and virtue,
these blessings increase, namely:
longevity, beauty, happiness, and strength.

Some preachers hold the view that a preoccupation with prolonging life is tantamount to craving, which entails clinging to the mind-body complex (*khandhā*). This, such preachers contend, is contrary to the teaching of the Buddha, which says: "Indulgence should not be given to life and to the mind-body complex (*khandha*)." In pursuance of such contentions they practised severe austerities or self-mortification by denying themselves food, clothing, or shelter from the ravages of weather such as sun, wind, rain, frost, etc. Such practices afford only a temporary means of dispelling such clinging (*upādāna*) and not a means of overcoming forever the fetter of clinging (*upādāna-saṃyojana*). They are just like the effort made during the current year in cutting down trees and clearing a plot of land of weeds and jungle bush. This effort, however, helps to promote a new and luxuriant growth of trees and jungle bushes on the same plot next year. Such austerity practices that we have mentioned above would, therefore, be helping in much the same way to promote a new and luxuriant growth of the fetter of clinging in the next existence.

The best way of overcoming forever this fetter of clinging is, metaphorically speaking, to use a hewing axe whose edge is as sharp as that of a razor blade. This hewing axe is called "insight knowledge" (*vipassanā-ñāṇa*), with which one should dig up and chop away the elements of one's mind-body complex, whether belonging to the present or to the future, until they are all, as it were, broken up into pieces and crushed up into the finest dust or powder. Being strong and healthy is one of the factors for a successful hewing-up and chopping-away of the fetter of clinging to the mind-body complex. This constitutes the second attribute for winning the higher knowledge of the Noble Ones. Therefore, anyone who makes the effort to attain the higher knowledge of the Noble Ones should strive hard to fulfil this requirement to be healthy and strong until one reaches the goal of one's endeavours.

Here ends the description of the second attribute.

The Third Attribute

With regard to the third attribute, the Buddha has made the following declaration in the *Aṅguttara Nikāya*:

> *Asaṭho hoti amāyāvī yathābhūtaṃ attānaṃ āvikattā satthari vā viññūsu vā sabrahmacārīsu.*

Meaning: "He is not sly or cunning. He is forthright and candid in dealing either with me (the Buddha) or his fellow disciples who are his superiors in wisdom." In the wider sense, it means that an aspirant to the higher knowledge of the Noble Ones should make manifest, without reserve or concealment, all those behaviours, plans, thoughts, ideas, and mental tendencies that are discreditable. He should also be open, without reserve or concealment, possessing all those behaviours, plans, thoughts, ideas, and mental tendencies that are admirable. He should not, in the very least, be sly and cunning by:

(a) Pretending to know what he does not actually know
(b) Pretending to have seen what he has not actually seen
(c) Pretending to know more while he actually knows less
(d) Pretending to be sharp-witted while he is actually dull-witted

All that is herein meant is that he must have a heart that is honest, upright, and pure.

Here ends the description of the third attribute.

The Fourth Attribute

With regard to the fourth attribute, the Buddha has declared as follows:

> *Āraddhaviriyo viharati akusalānaṃ dhammānaṃ pahānāya kusalānaṃ dhammānaṃ upasampadāya thāmavā daḷhaparakkamo anikkhittadhuro kusalesu dhammesu.*

Meaning: "He dwells always devoting his energy to dispelling evil and unwholesome characteristics and developing pure and wholesome characteristics. He is possessed of vigour and makes strong effort. He never relinquishes his responsibility to uphold the four kinds of virtue or wholesome characteristics."

He is endowed with such extraordinary keenness of mind, body, and energy as would enable him to: (1) dispel forever almost overnight, in this very lifetime, all unwholesome characteristics such as ignorance of the Four Noble Truths (*avijjā*) and craving (*taṇhā*); and (2) acquire and attain the wholesome characteristics that would lead him to (a) rebirth in blissful sensuous planes (*kāma-kusala*), (b) rebirth in fine-material spheres (*mahaggata-kusala*), and (c) attain the Supramundane Path and Fruition (*lokuttarakusala*).

A person who, due to a snakebite and the spread of snake venom all over his body, has fallen into a swoon and deep coma that puts a stop to all the faculties of seeing and breathing cannot be regarded to have passed the danger, or to being completely saved:

1. When he starts to breathe falteringly again as the first reaction to antivenom treatment administered to him
2. When next he rolls feebly from side to side
3. When next he recovers his eyesight
4. When next the snake venom recedes from the head down to the mid-regions
5. When next the snake venom recedes from the mid-section of the body to the lower regions
6. When next the snake venom recedes from the knees down to the lower limbs.

He can only be deemed to have passed the danger, or to have become completely safe, when the snake venom has been completely discharged from the opening caused by the original snakebite.

Just as the victim of a snakebite in the above simile cannot be regarded as having passed the danger, or as completely safe, from the mere fact that he has recovered his breathing faculty, the first reaction to antivenom treatment administered to him, even so, a person who, as a layman, is overwhelmed with the venom of sensual delights (*kāma-guṇa*) and the venom of hindrances (*nīvaraṇa*), cannot yet be regarded as safe by the mere fact that he is established in the purity of morality (*sīla-visuddhi*). Nor can he yet be regarded as safe just because, by renouncing the world and becoming a hermit or monk, he has practised austerities and established himself in the thirteen ascetic means of purification (*dhutaṅga*). He would be just like the aforesaid snakebite victim who is at the stage of rolling feebly from side to side.

When such a person becomes firmly established in morality and austerity practices, he approaches respectfully and waits upon a competent teacher of insight practice (*vipassanā*) from whom he takes practical lessons as a devout pupil. This he does by going to a place of solitude and quietude and assiduously applying himself to the practice of insight meditation. By means of sustained and arduous practice, he would realize, with clear comprehension, all groups of physical and mental phenomena and the process of their arising and passing away in his mind-body complex (*khandhā*). At this stage he resembles the victim of a snakebite who has recovered from the state of delirium and regained his eyesight. The mere regaining of eyesight should not be regarded as having recovered from the lethal effect of the snake venom. In the present age, there are quite a number of people resorting to jungle fastnesses and solitude in both Upper and Lower Burma, and who are entering upon insight practice in real earnest. They have not even reached the stage similar to that of regaining eyesight by the snake-bitten person.

When insight knowledge (*vipassanā-ñāṇa*) becomes highly developed and the stage of a stream-winner (*sotāpanna*) is reached, the insight trainee (*yogī*) resembles the snakebite victim in whom the snake venom has receded from the head.

When one reaches the stage of a once-returner (*sakadāgāmī*), one resembles the snakebite victim in whom the lethal effect of the snake venom has receded from the mid-section of the body downward.

When one reaches the stage of a non-returner (*anāgāmī*), one resembles the snakebite victim in whom the lethal effect of the snakebite has disappeared from above the knees.

When one reaches the stage of arahantship (*arahatta*), one resembles the snakebite victim from whom the whole mass of snake venom has been totally discharged from the whole system of the body through the opening caused by the original snakebite, leaving such a victim completely cured of all kinds of diseases and ailments due to the lethal effect of the snakebite.

So until such a stage of complete recovery and cure from the lethal effect of snake venom and all its consequent diseases and ailments is reached, it is appropriate for the victim of a snakebite to ignore all pressing problems other than the vital problem of curing the lethal effect of snake venom. His worries, his anxieties, and his energies should be devoted day and night to none other than curing the lethal effects of snakebite.

In like manner, people who are overwhelmed with the deadly venom known as the fifteen-hundred defilements (*kilesā*) that bind them to the sphere of death should never rest, but make unrelenting effort. They should continue doing so until they are completely purged of such deadly defilements through the attainment of the Path (*magga*) and Fruition (*phala*), even though they may have already reached and acquired the eight attainments (*samāpatti*),[10] and the ten stages of insight knowledge (*vipassanā-ñāṇa*).[11]

Such people should consider themselves as being endowed with supreme good fortune in finding in this present lifetime a superb physician in the person of the Buddha and the wonderful remedies and sovereign medicines prescribed by him in the form of insight wisdom (*vipassanā-paññā*) and path wisdom (*maggapaññā*).

Here ends the description of the fourth attribute.

The Fifth Attribute

> *Paññavā hoti udayatthagāminiyā paññāya samannāgato ariyāya nibbedhikāya sammā dukkhakkhaya-gāminiyā.*

A wise man is he who is endowed with such outstanding and powerful insight that he is:

1. Capable of overtaking, or catching up with, the uninterrupted process of arising and dissolution (at a tremendously high frequency of about a thousand million cycles in a split second) of the physical and mental phenomena of one's own person or the person of others
2. Too noble and sacred to be regarded as just an ordinary human being or deity
3. Capable of destroying the erroneous view of the compactness of physical and mental phenomena (mind-body complex), just as the thunderbolt weapon (*vajira*) shatters and smashes into fragments and finest powder both the summit and the whole mass of a massive mountain
4. Capable of guiding suffering sentient beings unerringly along a path that has no bends, curves, or impediments, straight to the *summum bonum*, which is the place where ends all recurring sorrows and sufferings (*vaṭṭa-dukkha*).

This fifth attribute is inherent only in an individual whose rebirth consciousness is conditioned by the three noble roots, i.e., non-greed, non-aversion, and non-delusion (*ti-hetuka-puggala*). The individuals who are born without these root conditions (*ahetuka-puggala*) and those who are born with only two noble root-conditions, i.e., non-greed and non-aversion (*dvi-hetuka-puggala*) cannot be endowed with this fifth attribute. The person who is endowed with this attribute knows definitely that he is a "three-root-conditioned individual."

As we said earlier, the Buddha has declared that a person who is endowed with these attributes is capable of making a successful attempt and winning the higher knowledge of the Noble Ones in the present lifetime.

Here ends the description of the fifth attribute.

The Attributes of Supreme Effort

The effort made with unflinching determination characterized by the following affirmations is called the supreme effort (*padhāna*):

1. Gladly would I be reduced to bones
2. Gladly would I be reduced to sinews

3. Gladly would I be reduced to skin
4. Let my body's flesh and blood dry up if there came to be a vortex of energy so that I might win what has not yet been won by human strength, by human energy, by human striving.

The person who makes this affirmation, which is followed by an effort that matches it, is designated as *padhāniya.*

These five qualities, which are worthily attributable to such a person, are called the five attributes of supreme effort (*padhāniyaṅga*).

Here ends the brief exposition on the five kinds of higher knowledge and the five attributes of a person who can win them.

Three Kinds of Higher Knowledge of the Noble Ones

We propose now, for the benefit of insight trainees who aspire to make a successful attempt at winning the higher knowledge of the Noble Ones (*ariya-vijjā*), to describe briefly from amongst the five kinds of higher knowledge, the method of attaining the following three branches of higher knowledge of the Noble Ones:

1. Higher knowledge of the truth of impermanence (*anicca-vijjā*)
2. Higher knowledge of the truth of suffering (*dukkha-vijjā*)
3. Higher knowledge of the truth of impersonality and conditionality (*anatta-vijjā*)

The Matrix

1. This physical body has as its fundamental basis the four great primaries (*ayaṃ kāyo cātum-mahābhūtiko*)
2. Its whole interior is decorated with six kinds of clear and bright mirrorlike elements (*ayaṃ kāyo chappasāda-maṇḍo*)
3. It is a product of ten kinds of thermal conditions or temperature (*ayaṃ kāyo utūnaṃ udayo*)
4. It is perpetually supported by ten kinds of nutriment (*ayaṃ kāyo āhārehi thambhito*)
5. It has the characteristic of origination in an uninterrupted process (*ayaṃ kāyo jātidhammo*)
6. It has the characteristic of decaying momentarily in a process (*ayaṃ kāyo jarādhammo*)

7. It has the characteristic of momentarily dying in a process (*ayaṃ kāyo maraṇadhammo*)
8. It has no enduring quality (*ayaṃ kāyo anicco*)
9. It is a sheer mass of suffering, unaccompanied by bliss (*ayaṃ kāyo dukkho*)
10. It is void of a self (*ayaṃ kāyo anattā*)

This is the matrix (*iti ayaṃ mātikā*).

First Item of the Matrix

The Four Great Primaries

The four great primaries (*mahābhūtā*) referred to in the above-mentioned matrix are: (1) the earth element (*paṭhavī-dhātu*), (2) the water element (*āpo-dhātu*), (3) the fire element (*tejo-dhātu*), and (4) the wind element (*vāyo-dhātu*). Of these four:

1. The characteristic of hardness (*kakkhaḷa-bhāva*), or of softness (*mudu-bhāvo*), is indeed the genuine earth element in the ultimate sense
2. The characteristic of cohesiveness (*ābandhana*), or of liquidity (*paggharaṇa*), is indeed the genuine water element in the ultimate sense
3. The characteristic of heat (*uṇha-bhāva*), or of coldness (*sīta-bhāvo*), is indeed the genuine fire element in the ultimate sense
4. The characteristic of support or tension (*vitthambhana*), or of motion (*samudīraṇa*), is indeed the wind element in the ultimate sense

These are aphorisms that should be thoroughly studied and learnt by heart.

We shall now expound the four great primaries, i.e., the elements of earth, water, wind, and fire, in such a way that each of them may be comprehended with higher knowledge (*vijjā-ñāṇa*).

Genuine Earth Element in the Ultimate Sense

The genuine earth element in the ultimate sense (*paramattha*) means the mere characteristic, quality, or function (*kiriyā*) of hardness, which has no core, substance, or mass of the size even of a hundred thousandth part of an atom. This quality of hardness in the ultimate sense is, however, present in all parts of things and objects including:

(a) The clear, transparent waters of rivers, streams, springs, fountains, water-holes, etc.
(b) Sunrays, moonbeams, starlight, firelight, or the bright radiance of a ruby
(c) The sound of bells or of rotating brass gongs that floats near or afar
(d) The gentle breeze, the soft wind, the gale or storm, and the fragrant or foul smells that pervade the air far or near.

The Potency of the Earth Element

As mentioned above, all things and objects such as water, light, sound, etc., are replete with the earth element. This finding is supported by the fact that:

1. The four great primaries are inseparable and are complementary to one another (*avinibbhoga-vutti*)
2. The Buddha has declared:

   Ekaṃ mahā-bhūtaṃ paṭicca tayo mahā-bhūtā,
   tayo mahā-bhūte paṭicca ekaṃ mahā-bhūtaṃ, dve
   mahā-bhūte paṭicca dve mahā-bhūtā.

   "One great primary is the conditioning factor of the other three great primaries; the other three great primaries are the conditioning factors of one great primary; any two great primaries are the conditioning factors of the other two great primaries." (Paṭṭhāna I § 53)
3. The commentaries say the earth element has the function of receiving, or supporting (*sampaṭicchana-rasā*) the water element, the wind element, and the fire element
4. The characteristics of water, fire, and wind are such that they cannot come into existence without the earth element as their support

This is evidence supported by scriptural authority.

Evidence Supported By Characteristics

It is evident that in a mass of water, or in a mass of wind, the lower layers, in succession, support the upper ones. This state of support is not the characteristic of the water element because cohesiveness is the only characteristic of the water element. This state of support is also not the characteristic of the fire element because heat or cold is the only characteristic of the fire element. This state of support, therefore, concerns the characteristics of the earth element and the wind element because this state is possible only by a combination of hardness with support or tension. Of these two, hardness is called the earth element in the ultimate sense, and support or tension is called the wind element in the ultimate sense. Again, of these two, support or tension, which is called the wind element, has to depend on hardness, which is called the earth element, without which the wind element, by itself, cannot exist. You should try to see the difference between the characteristic of hardness and that of support or tension. In this way you should understand with clear comprehension that the earth element, in the ultimate sense, is in both water and wind elements. This can be achieved by observing the characteristic of hardness (*kakkhaḷa-lakkhaṇa*) in both wind and water in their respective strengths.

Characteristics of Hardness in Light, etc.

Although the characteristic of hardness exists in light such as sunrays, etc., in sounds, such as the sound of a bell, etc., and in smells, such as fragrant smells, these objects, according to their nature, are very weak in the characteristic of hardness, and as such, proof of its existence by characteristics alone is impossible. Evidence of its presence can be produced in the form of scriptural authority only. The examples of transparent water, wind, moonbeams, sounds, and smells are given here just to make the following clear:

1. The mere quality or characteristic of hardness is the genuine earth element in the ultimate sense
2. The genuine earth element has no core, substance or mass with the size even of a hundred thousandth part of an atom

This earth element, which is without a core, substance, or mass, is merely a quality or characteristic of hardness. It is said to be hard if the strength of hardness is high, and soft if the strength of hardness is low.

One should understand the gradual escalation of the degree of hardness or softness of this earth element, and the difference between hardness in the highest strength, as that of the diamond (*vajira*) at one extreme, and the hardness of the weakest strength as that of a component material unit of the moonbeam at the other extreme. The quality or characteristic of hardness in this earth element should be contemplated in terms of ultimate realities (*paramattha-dhamma*) and not in terms of common-sense perceptions. In the latter case, the element of hardness will not be detected in such rays of light as the moonbeam.

When hundreds of thousands of millions and tens of thousands of millions of units of the earth element in the ultimate sense, which in reality is a mere characteristic of hardness, are bonded together in one mass by the element of cohesiveness (*āpo-dhātu*), a thing or object with shape and mass, which is called an "atom" (*anu-myū*) comes into existence. When hundreds of thousands of millions and tens of thousands of millions of units of such atoms are again bonded together, a speck of organic matter called "flea" or "bug" develops. Thus it should be realized by a series of multiplications how:

(a) In the world of beings, the massive body of the King of the Titans (*asurinda*) measuring four-thousand eight-hundred *yojanas* (a *yojana* is a distance of about seven miles) is built up

(b) In the case of visible external objects with form (*bahiddhā saṇṭhāna*) such as the massive mass of Mount Meru, which measures twice eighty-four thousand *yojanas* in height, or of the Great Earth, which measures two-hundred and forty thousand *yojanas* in depth, are built up.

So this quality or characteristic of hardness, which is called the earth element, forms the fundamental basis of all things animate or inanimate, beginning with the minutest objects such as a flea or an atom. There is no element other than the earth element from which material things could be derived. The elements of water, fire, and wind have to depend on it for their existence. Thus the great importance of the function of the earth element should be understood.

If you desire to contemplate the earth element only in its ultimate sense, you should isolate the mere quality or characteristic of hardness, having neither form nor mass with a size even as small as that of an atom. You will then perceive the quality or characteristic of hardness just as if it were an image reflected in a mirror or on the surface of placid water. If, however, during insight contemplation on the great primary elements, an idea of long or short, big or small, solid or compact, creeps into your mental vision, it is but an indication that the object of contemplation is not the genuine earth element in the ultimate sense. In such a case, the contemplation should be regarded as being fouled or mixed up with the concept of forms (*saṇṭhāna-paññatti*) or of material substances with dimensions. When the earth element in the ultimate sense is confused with the concept of forms or mass, a clear comprehension of the process of arising and dissolution (of mental and physical phenomena) will not be possible in the next (advanced) stage of contemplation.

It should he noted that in giving instructions in the practice of contemplation of the four great primaries to the Venerable Ānanda, the Venerable Puṇṇa Mahāthera gave this example of a reflex image in the mirror. This example of a reflex image in the mirror was instrumental in the Venerable Ānanda's becoming a stream-winner (*sotāpanna*).

If a person can clearly comprehend the quality or characteristic of hardness called the earth element in the ultimate sense, without mixing it with the vision of any substance even as small as an atom during his exercise of contemplation on any objects, both animate and inanimate, it will be easy for him to clearly comprehend the earth element in all lesser animate and inanimate objects. The images of forests, trees, or mountains reflected in a mirror or a sheet of placid water may appear as big as Mount Meru, but when conditions favourable for their disappearance or destruction arise, they are bound to disappear or become destroyed more than a hundred times within the period occupied by a wink or a flash of lightning. The reason is that they are devoid of a core or substance even as small as an atom. In the same way he will be able to see the signs and characteristics of a similar disappearance or destruction of the earth element (*paṭhavī-dhātu*) in the ultimate sense, which pervades the entire mass of, and is as big as, Mount Meru, as it also is devoid of a core or substance even as small as an atom.

When a person contemplates the genuine earth element within his own body for the sake of enlightenment, he should contemplate his body part-by-part so that the circumscribed area of his investigation may be commensurate with his power of concentration and contemplation. When he contemplates a part, for instance his head, he should contemplate it right through without making a distinction between the interior and the exterior.

During such contemplation, the element of colour might intervene and lead him astray. The idea of shapes, forms, or mass, i.e. pictorial ideas (*saṇṭhāna-paññatti*) is also likely to intervene and lead him astray. In such instances, he should persistently bring his mind back to full awareness. In applying mindfulness to the lower portion of his body down to the soles of his feet, a person should also contemplate his body part-by-part so that each circumscribed area of his investigation may be commensurate with his power of concentration and contemplation. When the whole body is fully covered by this exercise, the contemplation of the genuine earth element in the head will make him realize simultaneously the same element in all other parts of the body down to the soles of his feet. If a person is successful in realizing the genuine earth element in regard to his own body, it is as good as realizing the same element in regard to the bodies of all other beings in the infinite universe and world systems. A successful realization of the genuine earth element will make it much more easy to realize with deep penetration all other elements in the internal (*ajjhattika*) sphere, such as the water element, the fire element, the wind element, the eye element, the ear element, etc., and also the elements of the external (*bahiddhā*) sphere such as the visible object (*rūpa-dhātu*), the sound element (*sadda-dhātu*), etc.

Here ends the brief exposition of the method of contemplating the earth element, called paṭhavī-dhātu, with successful penetration.

Genuine Water Element in the Ultimate Sense

In the ultimate sense, "water element" means the quality of cohesiveness. When this quality assumes a position of strength and vigour, it becomes the water element (*āpo-dhātu*) having the quality of wetness or liquidity (*paggharaṇa*). This water element in the ultimate sense, which is the mere quality of cohesiveness (*ābandhana-kiriyā*), is devoid of a core or substance lacking even the size or dimensions of a hundred thousandth part of an atom. This water element binds together the other elements, namely, earth element, wind element, and fire element, which coexist with it in the same material unit (*kalāpa*). These elements are interdependent, coexistent and mutually supporting. So when the water element disappears, those other elements also disappear instantaneously.

The above treatise explains the important contribution made by the water element (*āpo-dhātu*) in the formation of a material unit.

Just on account of this water element, the material groups can exist in this world in various forms, shapes, and solid masses with either big or small sizes ranging from an electrical particle (*paramāṇu-myū*) to:

(a) The massive body of the King of the Titans (*asurinda*) in the world of beings and
(b) Mount Meru, the circumjacent mountains (Mount Cakkavāḷa), or the Great Earth in the physical universe.[12]

Apart from this water element, there is no other element that can hold the elements together as particles or solid objects. If the quality of cohesiveness in Mount Meru, which measures twice eighty four thousand *yojanas* in height, were destroyed, that Mount Meru itself would disappear instantaneously. If the quality of cohesiveness in the circumjacent mountains, which measure twice eighty-two thousand *yojanas* in height, were destroyed, the circumjacent mountains themselves would disappear instantaneously. If the quality of cohesiveness in the Great Earth were destroyed, the Great Earth itself would disappear instantaneously, leaving only an open space in its place.

Why? Because in the absence of the quality of cohesiveness, or binding force, the whole mass of the earth element, the fire element, and the wind element, which underlie or manifest themselves as the massive Mount Meru, circumjacent mountains, or the Great Earth, would be deprived of mutually supporting coexistence and interdependence and thus disintegrate instantaneously. With the exception of *Nibbāna* (unoriginated and uncreated), all the other ultimate realities (*paramattha-dhamma*), which have the signs and characteristics of being formed or conditioned (*saṅkhata-lakkhaṇa*), cannot remain even for the wink of an eye or a flash of lightning if they are without such support or help.

If one desires to exercise contemplation on the water element underlying Mount Meru, circumjacent mountains, and the Great Earth in the ultimate sense, one should contemplate the quality of cohesiveness only, without confusing it with the quality of hardness that is inherent only in the earth element. During such contemplation the element of colour and pictorial ideas are prone to stand in the way.

If the determining knowledge of phenomena (*dhamma-vavatthāna-ñāṇa*) is obstructed by colour and pictorial ideas, a clear comprehension of the process of arising and dissolution (of mental and physical phenomena) will not be possible in the next higher stage of contemplation. A realization of the three characteristics of existence, i.e., (1) impermanence (*anicca*), (2) suffering (*dukkha*), and (3) impersonality and conditionality (*anattā*) in their truest sense, is possible only when the ultimate realities (*paramattha-dhamma*) are fully grasped with clear comprehension.

As in the case of the earth element, a person who understands with clear comprehension that the water element is a mere quality or characteristic of cohesiveness will also understand with clear comprehension that there is neither a core nor substance whatsoever even in Mount Meru and the Great Earth, just as there is neither a core nor substance in the images of rain, clouds, sun, moon, or trees reflected in a mirror or on the surface of placid waters. When the water element in Mount Meru and the Great Earth is fully comprehended, the comprehension of the same element with insight in all earthly and heavenly beings will become very easy. What matters most is to realize the water element in its ultimate sense in all sentient beings. We introduce such massive objects as Mount Meru and the Great Earth in our explanation in order to pave the way for readily understanding the water element as a mere quality of cohesiveness in the formation of living beings. One should first realize this element with respect to one's own person from the top of one's head to the soles of one's feet and only then contemplate the water element in respect to other beings.

Here ends the brief exposition of the method of contemplating the water element, called āpo-dhātu, which leads to penetrative insight.

Comprehending the Fire Element

The quality of heat or cold is that which provides incubating warmth to promote the growth, energy, and strength of the other three great primary elements with which it is coexistent in the same material unit (*kalāpa*). The dual energy of heat and cold have in each the incubating warmth that promotes the growth, energy, and strength of the other great primary elements with which it is coexistent in the same material unit. Eggs laid by a hen in a nest can grow in strength and energy in gradual stages and hatch into chickens only if the mother hen constantly sits and imparts her bodily warmth to them. If the mother hen does not sit to impart her bodily warmth, such eggs will not be able to develop into chickens. Instead, those eggs will become rotten as soon as the bodily warmth received during the incubation period in the mother's womb becomes exhausted.

In this simile the fire element resembles the mother hen and the other three coexisting elements of earth, wind, and water resemble the yolk of an egg. Only in combination with the fire element can hardness (earth element) come into effective existence; only in combination with the fire element can cohesion (water element) come into effective existence; and only in combination with the fire element, can vibration (wind element) come into effective existence. They cannot come into effective existence without the fire element.

Water in the great ocean, water in the seas, and water that supports this Great Earth are dependent on the (cold) fire element. They have to continue their existence subject to its control. Mount Meru, Mountain of the Universe, and the Great Earth are also dependent on the (cold) fire element. In contemplating the fire element only, without mixing it up with the other elements, one should contemplate only the quality of coldness in the cold objects and only the quality of heat in hot objects. The idea of shapes, form, or mass (pictorial ideas) should not be allowed to intervene and lead one astray. The fact that the fire element in its ultimate sense is devoid of a core, essence, or substance the size of even an atom is quite obvious. For this reason, when the fire element is comprehended with purity of understanding and clarity of vision, one will realize that there is neither a core nor substance of any size or dimension in that element, just as the images of the sun, moon, clouds, and rain that are reflected in a mirror or on the surface of placid water do not contain any substance although they appear to be massive in one's perception. In contemplating the fire element in one's own body, one should do so part-by-part so that each area may be contained within the range of one's contemplative capacity.

If one is capable of clearly comprehending the fire element in one's own body, one becomes capable of clearly comprehending the fire element in all other beings of the infinite universe.

Here ends the brief exposition of the method of contemplating the fire element with penetration.

The Wind Element in the Ultimate Sense

A volume of flame or smoke contains within it the wind element, which, by virtue of the wind element, is the propagating agency for the perpetuation of the fire element itself. On account of that wind element the propagation of the fire element becomes evident in various forms such as:

The spread of fire
The radiation of heat
The radiation of light
The upward spread of lively flames
The emission of smoke
The spread of new fires in succession

By the same token, this wind element is what causes the vibration of the fire element, which, in the ultimate sense, is the mere quality of heat or cold. By virtue of this factor, any spark of fire placed together with an inflammable object is liable to spread throughout the whole area of that object. If, due to weakness of that vibrating factor, the fire does not spread, external help is rendered to it by producing the vibrating factor in the form of a current of air by fanning or propelling air through a funnel or tube.

Where there is the quality or characteristic of heat, there are bound to be elements of heat-vibration and heat-energy. Likewise the quality of coldness is accompanied always by the elements of cold-vibration and cold-energy. It should be remembered that the quality of heat or cold is one characteristic and its vibration and energy are different characteristics. The quality of heat or cold is the fire element in the ultimate sense, while vibration or energy is the wind element in the ultimate sense. This quality of vibration or energy is deemed to be a sinew of strength of the earth element, the water element, and the fire element, which are coexistent with it in the same material unit (*kalāpa*). These coexisting great primary elements have to accompany the vibration or energy of the wind element wherever it goes. When the strength of this vibration or energy grows to excess, it develops into a storm. As this energy has the quality or characteristic of support or resistance, such as may be observed in air mattresses or air pillows, the scriptural texts have described it as having the characteristic of support (*vitthambhana-lakkhaṇa*). The coldness quality of the fire element (*sīta-tejo-dhātu*), which is inherent in the massive Mount Meru, the circumjacent mountains, and the Great Earth, is capable of developing, from moment to moment, until the final destruction or cataclysm of this Great Earth. You are hereby urged to contemplate until this element is fully comprehended.

There are such processes of evolution as the growth and spread throughout the whole body of mind produced material units (*cittaja-rūpa-kalāpa*) and of temperature produced material units (*utuja-rūpa-kalāpa*), occasioned by the arising on the physical heart base of a certain unit of consciousness. There are such processes of evolution as the growth and spread throughout the whole body of nutriment when material food reaches the stomach. There are such processes of evolution as the steady growth and propagation of the physical body of living beings, each beginning with its nucleic (*kalala*) fluid. There are also such processes of evolution as the growth and propagation of trees, plants, creepers, shrubs, and grasses, beginning with sprouts and shoots. All of these processes are due to the generating function of the wind element.

You should contemplate this wind element in the massive Mount Meru, in the circumjacent mountains, in the Great Earth and in all things animate and inanimate until you observe with clear comprehension that the whole mass of these objects is filled with a seething mass of microscopic eruptions and combustions. You should begin by observing the state of motion and unrest subjectively with regard to your own body, and then observe the similar state in all other objects, both animate and inanimate. With regard to your own body, contemplation should cover the whole of it from the top of your head to the soles of your feet. You will find that this element is, as we have said earlier, devoid of a core or substance of a size even as small as that of an atom, and as such you should comprehend it merely as an image such as that of a man reflected on the surface of placid water or in a mirror. During the exercise of contemplation, the pictorial idea or the familiar concepts of shapes, form or mass are likely to intervene and lead you astray from the right path. You should, in such cases, seek the aid of wisdom (*paññā*) and do away with this concept (*paññatti-dhamma*), which is a nonentity in the ultimate sense.

Here ends the brief exposition of the method of contemplating the wind element with successful penetration.

Interdependence Between Each of the Four Great Primaries

Hardness, cohesiveness, incubating warmth, and vibrating energy—each of these four great qualities or attributes is prominent by itself through its own feature or characteristic. They are coexistent as a single unit, based on the element of hardness, and so arise together, dissolve together, and exist together.

If hardness or the earth element is destroyed, the other three elements are also bound to be destroyed as they would be deprived of a basis for their existence.

Likewise, if cohesiveness or the water element is destroyed, all the other elements are also bound to be destroyed as they would be deprived of the binding force and mutual support.

If the fire element with its attribute of incubating warmth and vitalizing energy is destroyed, the other three elements are also bound to become destroyed and vanish, as they cannot exist in full complement by themselves.

If vibration/compression or the wind element is destroyed, the remaining elements are also bound to be destroyed as they would be deprived of their strength.

The fire element, with its attributes of heat or cold, can exist only in combination with the wind element with its attributes of generating energy or motion. If the wind element is absent, the fire element would be deprived of strength, and vanish instantaneously.

Likewise, if the wind element, with its attribute of compression that supports the quality of hardness of the earth element, is destroyed, the earth element would be deprived of its strength and thus be bound to die out.

Likewise, if the wind element, with its attribute of compression that supports the quality of cohesiveness of the water element is absent, the water element would be deprived of its strength and thus be bound to die out.

This is the explanation of the interdependence between each of the four great primaries and of the fact that the disappearance of one of them means the total disappearance of the others.

Beyond the Range of Speculative Thinking

The part played by the four great primaries in all things, animate or inanimate, is so great and wonderful as to be inconceivable (*acinteyya*), i.e., something beyond the range of speculative thinking or reasoning. Likewise psychic powers and forces involved in these elements are so tremendous as to be beyond the range of speculative thinking.

If one investigates and follows the method proclaimed by the Buddha, with penetrative insight and utmost striving, one can make a successful breakthrough and win the supramundane knowledge of the Noble Ones (*lokuttara-ariya-vijjā*). If, on the other hand, one investigates and follows the method adopted by sorcerers (*vijjā*), one can make a successful breakthrough and win the mundane occult and magical powers with tremendous possibilities (*lokiya-gandhāri-vijjā*).

If a successful breakthrough can be made by following a mediocre method, one can still achieve a higher knowledge in: (a) medical science (medicine), (b) chemical science (chemistry), or (c) mechanical science (engineering).

Of these four great primaries, the fire element is predominant and plays the leading role. The whole universe, comprising the Great Earth, with its constituents of land and water, with all things of colour and form, either animate or inanimate, are all the products of the fire element. The powers and forces of this element and their potentialities are within the range only of the supreme knowledge or omniscience (*sabbaññuta-ñāṇa*) of the Supremely Enlightened Buddhas.

Here ends the amplified meaning of the term cātum-mahābhūtiko expressed in the first item of the matrix.

Second Item of the Matrix

The Six Mirrorlike Elements

In the second item of the matrix the following description has been given: "Its (the body's) whole interior is decorated with six kinds of clear and bright mirrorlike elements (*chappasāda-maṇḍo*)." It may be pointed out in this connection that according to the rules of grammar and etymology three Pāḷi words, *pasādo, maṇḍo,* and *accho* convey the same meaning, i.e., "mirrorlike clearness."

Of the three the word *maṇḍo* is absorbed into the Burmese language as *phan* (crystal) and *mand* (glass), of which the present day Burmese expression *hman* (glass or mirror) is a derivative.

This glass element (*chappasāda-maṇḍo*) is of two kinds, namely: (1) the temperature-produced glass element (*utuja-maṇḍa-dhātu*), and (2) the volition (*kamma*) produced glass element (*kammaja-maṇḍa-dhātu*). Of these two, the glassware that is fashioned at the glass industrial quarters of Rangoon and Mandalay, i.e., optical glasses, also microscope and telescope lenses, fall within the category of temperature-produced glass elements. However, the glass element, formed within the bodies of sentient beings, falls within the category of volition (*kamma*) produced glass elements. In the latter category there are six kinds of glass elements as follows:

1. The mirrorlike element, called the eye (*cakkhu-pasāda*)
2. The mirrorlike element, called the ear (*sota-pasāda*)
3. The mirrorlike element, called the nose (*ghāṇa-pasāda*)
4. The mirrorlike element, called the tongue (*jivhā-pasāda*)
5. The mirrorlike element, called the body (*kāya-pasāda*)
6. The mirrorlike element, called the mind-base (*manāyatana*)

As to the place of their location:

1. The mirrorlike element of the eye lies within the eye-organ
2. The mirrorlike element of the ear lies within the ear-organ
3. The mirrorlike element of the nose lies within the nose-organ
4. The mirrorlike element of the tongue lies in the surface of the tongue-organ
5. The mirrorlike element of the body lies throughout the body
6. The mirrorlike element of the mind lies within the heart.

To the insight-trainee (*yogī*) who clearly comprehends the six mirrorlike elements, this body of five aggregates very much resembles an exceedingly bright and clear mass or pillar of crystal or glass.

In the synopsis of "door" (*dvāra-saṅgaha*) in the *Comprehensive Manual of Abhidhamma* (*Abhidhammatthasaṅgaha*) the six glassy-bright elements are also called "doors" (*dvāra*).

Two Kinds of Door

The term *dvāra* means "door" or "opening," which is of two kinds, namely: (1) space-opening (*ākāsa-dvāra*) and (2) glass-door opening (*maṇḍa-dvāra*). In the houses of persons of affluence there are two kinds of door. The first kind comprises doors fixed at openings for the entry or exit of people, and doors fixed at openings for the entry or exit of air. The second kind of door has no opening, but is fitted with plate glass and is called "door of transparency" or "door of light."

In the case of the doors that are fitted with plate glass, the images of things and objects that are far or near, such as the sun, moon, stars, heavenly bodies, clouds, blue sky, land masses, water collections, forests, mountains, trees, houses and housing sites, monasteries, reservoirs, pagodas, shrines, etc., are reflected in their original shapes, forms, and colours in such plate glass. The occupants of the house, even when staying inside it, can see all the images of the sun, moon, sunlight, moonlight, etc., in their entirety, as reflected in the plate glass. When looking from the outside into the house through such a plate glass door, they can also see the objects inside the house in their entirety. All sunlight, moonlight, and lamplight, indeed, are associates of the plate glass of such doors. Just as the big house mentioned in the above simile has two kinds of door all over the place, even so the body of each man, deity, bullock, buffalo, elephant, horse, fowl, or bird has also two kinds of door, namely: (1) space-door and (2) glass-door.

The Space-Door

The space-door comprises: (1) the group known as the "nine openings," including the mouth opening, the throat orifice, the aperture of the nose through which nasal discharges are expelled, the eye-openings through which tears are discharged, etc.; and (2) the group known as the "ninety-nine thousand minute orifices or pores of the skin."

The aforesaid volition-produced mirrorlike elements of the interior (*ajjhatta-kammaja-dhātu-maṇḍa*) are called:

1. The mirrorlike element of the sensitive eye-organ
2. The mirrorlike element of the sensitive ear-organ
3. The mirrorlike element of the sensitive nose-organ
4. The mirrorlike element of the sensitive tongue-organ
5. The mirrorlike element of the sensitive body-organ
6. The mirrorlike element of the mind-base

These are, however, not doors with space openings. They are mere mirrorlike glazed doors admitting light and reflecting images. The functions of these six volition-produced mirrorlike elements may be illustrated as follows. Suppose there is a manor house with its roof, walls, and window fittings replete with crystal and plate glass. In the middle of that manor house there is also an incomparable and exceedingly clear and transparent crystal ball. The images of cloud banks and cloud drifts, of the sun, moon, stars, and heavenly bodies, and of birds flying past in the sky, come through the transparent glass roof, and are reflected on the crystal ball. The images of the sun and of the moon are reflected simultaneously on the glass roof and on the crystal ball. Likewise, the images of all objects in the sky above are reflected both on the glass roof and on the crystal ball inside the manor house all at once.

In the same way the images of the objects on the east side of the manor house are reflected both on the plate glass of the windows on the east side and on the crystal ball in the middle of the manor house simultaneously. The images of objects on the west, south and north sides are similarly reflected. The images of objects below that manor house are also reflected both on the transparent glass flooring and on the crystal ball in the middle of the building.

Corresponding to the crystal ball inside the manor house of the above simile, there exists within the heart inside this physical body a great crystal ball, called the mind-base (*mano*). In the Book of Ones in the *Aṅguttara Nikāya*, the Buddha has declared: "This consciousness, O monks, sparkles aglow with brilliance" (*pabhassaram-idaṃ bhikkhave cittaṃ*). The mirrorlike element of mind-base, which is called *mano*, therefore sparkles aglow with brilliance.

Even in the case of consciousness without root conditions (*ahetuka-citta*), a mental picture of past events reflects in that mirrorlike element of one's mind-base whenever any particular experience of one's past lifetime is adverted to.

In such cases, the clearness of reflection on the mirrorlike mind-base without root-conditions is surpassed by the clearness of reflection on the mind-base with two (noble) root conditions (*dvihetuka*), namely, non-greed and non-hate. Similarly, the clearness of reflection on the mind-base with two (noble) root-conditions is surpassed by the clearness of reflection on the mind-base with three (noble) root conditions (*tihetuka*), namely, non-greed, non-hate, and non-delusion.

In terms of planes of existence (*bhūmi*), the clearness of reflection on the mind-base in the human-world with three (noble) root-conditions, is surpassed by the clearness of reflection on the mind-base of the earth deities. The clearness of reflection on the mind-base of the earth deities is, in turn, surpassed by that of the deities of the *Tāvatiṃsa* heaven, which, in turn, is surpassed by that of the deities of the *Yāmā* heaven, and so on and so forth until the highest plane of existence (*bhavagga*) is reached.

In terms of individuals (*puggala*), the clearness of reflection on the mind-base of worldlings (*puthujjana*) is surpassed by the clearness of reflection on the mind-base of ordinary enlightened Noble Disciples (*pakati-sāvaka-bodhi*), which is surpassed in succession by clearness of reflection on the mind-bases, respectively, of the great enlightened Noble Disciples (*mahā-sāvaka-bodhi*), of the Individual or Silent Buddhas (*pacceka-bodhi*), and of the Supremely Enlightened or Omniscient Buddhas (*sabbaññuta-bodhi*). Of these, the mind-base of the Supremely Enlightened Buddhas has reached the summit, beyond which there is no room for further progress.

In infinities (*ananta*) such as universes, world systems, sentient beings, formations or conditioned things (*saṅkhāra*), designations or concepts (*paññatti-dhamma*), and the single element of unconditioned Nibbāna (*nibbāna-eka*), there is none that does not reflect on the mind-base of the Supremely Enlightened One, the Omniscient One. All objects must reflect on that mind-base, which may be likened to the crystal ball inside the aforesaid manor house. The five physical sense organs of "sensitive materiality" (*pasāda-rūpa*) comprising:

the sensitive eye-organ (*cakkhu-pasāda*),
the sensitive ear-organ (*sota-pasāda*),
the sensitive nose-organ (*ghāṇa-pasāda*),
the sensitive tongue-organ (*jivhā-pasāda*),
the sensitive body-organ (*kāya-pasāda*),

are just like the plate glass fitted on the six sides (east, west, north, south, above and below) of the manor house allegorized above.

All visible objects with shape and form are bound to arrive at their twin destinations, namely sensitive eye-organ and mind-base (*manāyatana*). All sounds are bound to arrive at their twin destinations, namely sensitive ear-organ and mind-base. All smells or odours are bound to arrive at their twin destinations, namely sensitive nose-organ and mind-base. All tastes are bound to arrive at their twin destinations, namely sensitive tongue-organ and mind-base. All sense of touch involving the elements of heat or cold, hardness or softness, is bound to arrive at its twin destinations, namely sensitive body-organ that is spread all over the body and the mind-base. All other mental-objects (*dhammārammaṇa*) are bound to arrive at their single destination, namely the mind-base.

Thus, when one looks up in the sky with one's eyes, the image of the moon, which is shining aglow with radiance and splendour, is reflected in the sensitive eye-organ while another image with the same attributes is simultaneously reflected in the mind-base, which is within the heart (*hadaya-vatthu*). The two images therefore have to appear at the two different places with neither one preceding or succeeding the other.

Simultaneity in the Occurrence of Events

The example of two events occurring at the same time with neither one preceding or succeeding the other may be observed in the act of a bird alighting on the bough of a tree. Both the bird and its shadow come in contact with the bough of the tree and its shadow simultaneously. It may also be observed in the act of a man and his image in a mirror, both smiling at the same time with neither one preceding or succeeding the other. It may also be observed in the aforesaid simile of the manor house that is fitted with plate glass windows on all sides and a huge crystal ball in the middle of it.

The huge image of the sun that rises in the east comes in through the plate glass window on the eastern wall of the manor house and reflects its shining splendour on the crystal ball in the middle of that manor house. By merely looking at this crystal ball without needing to look eastward, anyone can still see the huge image of the sun.

On the same analogy, when one looks up at the sky to see the moon with one's eyes, the image of the radiant moon comes in through the volition-produced mirrorlike element (*kammaja-maṇḍa-dhātu*), which is called the eye-organ, and reflects on the volition-produced mirrorlike element called the mind-base (*manāyatana*), which is located within the heart. Both reflections of the moon image on the mirrorlike elements of the eye-organ and mind-base take place simultaneously.

In the case of fading out or disappearance of moon images, however, there is a difference. The moon image that is reflected on the mirrorlike element of the eye-organ may have faded out, but the moon image that is reflected on the heart-base may not have done so and still lingers on. This fact is important and should be carefully observed until it is realized with penetrative insight.

If one thoroughly grasps this point, one will be able to realize with penetrative insight the same phenomenon in all six sense bases.

Contemplation of Impact on the Eye and Mind Bases

The reflection of that moon image on the mirrorlike elements of the eye-organ and heart-base makes an impact that is as tremendous as the striking of a thunderbolt. Likewise when one looks up at the sun in the sky, one image of the sun is reflected on the sensitive eye-organ and another similar image is reflected on the mirrorlike element of the mind-base. Both of these events occur simultaneously with neither one preceding nor succeeding the other. The same holds true when one looks at a tree. One image of the tree reflects on the sensitive eye-organ and another similar image reflects on the mirrorlike element of the mind-base. Both of these events occur at the same time.

In the case of seeing a person, one image of that person is reflected on the eye-base while another similar image is reflected on the mind-base at the same time. Such reflection makes an impact similar in power to the striking of a thunderbolt. It should be understood that the same is true of the reflecting of images of all visual objects on the eye-base and mind-base. Just as the conjunction of storm clouds produces flashes of lightning; just as a meteor hurtling through the air produces a shooting star; just as sound is produced by the clash of one hard object against another; just as sparks of fire are produced by a flint struck with steel; even so, the eye-consciousness element arises in a boiling-up process of the sensitive eye-organ as an aftereffect of the impact of an image, such as that of the moon, on the sensitive eye-organ, which is likened to the tremendous impact of a thunderbolt. It is called "eye-consciousness element" (*cakkhu-viññāṇa-dhātu*) because the impact takes place on the sensitive eye-organ. When the force of such an impact wears away, that element of eye-consciousness also dies out just like a spark of fire dying out. Due to the force of its impact on the mirrorlike element of the mind-base the process of thought moments (*vīthi-citta*) cognizing the visual object of the aforesaid moon arises in a boiling-up process. It is just like the material units (*kalāpa*) of a reverberant sound that arises when a bell or rotating brass gong is struck with a hammer or mallet. When the force of impact of the blow wears away, the reverberant sound also dies out. On the same analogy the process of eye-consciousness dies out when the force of impact, occasioned by the reflection of the image of the aforesaid moon, wears away. It should be understood that the same is true of image reflections of all other visual objects on the eye-base.

Here ends the exposition on the method of contemplating the point of conjunction of the three elements, namely: (1) the sensitive eye-organ, (2) visual object, and (3) eye-consciousness that would lead to attainment of insight-wisdom at one stroke.

Contemplation of Impact on the Ear and Mind Bases

The audible sound of rain, the sound of falling water, the sound of a drum, the sound of a bell, the voice of a man, the barking of a dog, the crowing of a cock, or the chirping of a bird, reflects with an impact both on the mirrorlike element called "sensitive ear-organ" and the mirrorlike element of the mind-base, which is located within the heart. Both events occur at the same time with neither one preceding nor succeeding the other. The force of such an impact is as tremendous as the striking of a thunderbolt. Due to the force of impact of that audible sound on the mirrorlike element of the sensitive ear-organ, a process of thought called "ear-consciousness" arises in a boiling-up manner. This consciousness is called the "ear-consciousness element" (*sota-viññāṇa-dhātu*) because the impact takes place on the sensitive ear-organ. When that sound ceases, such ear-consciousness also dies out and vanishes. Due to the force of impact on the mirrorlike element of the mind-base, the process of thought moments (*vīthi-citta*) cognizing such sound arises in a boiling-up process. As in the case of the sound of the bell in the example given above, that process of ear-consciousness dies out and vanishes when the force of impact of that sound wears away. It should be understood that the same is true of all kinds of sounds heard by the ear-organ.

Here ends the exposition on the method of contemplating the point of conjunction of the three elements, namely: (1) the sensitive ear-organ, (2) sound, and (3) ear-consciousness that would lead to attainment of insight-wisdom at one stroke.

Contemplation of Impact on the Other Bases

Consider the following two triads, namely:

1. The mirrorlike element at the sensitive nose-organ, called *ghāṇa-pasāda*
2. Various odours or smells, called *gandhārammaṇa*
3. Nose-consciousness element, called *ghāṇa-viññāṇa-dhātu*.

and

1. The mirrorlike element at the sensitive tongue-organ, called *jivhā-pasāda*
2. Various tastes such as sweetness or sourness, called *rasārammaṇa*
3. Tongue-consciousness element, called *jivhā-viññāṇa-dhātu*.

The point of conjunction of each triad, together with the process of their arising and dissolution, should be contemplated as in the case of the sensitive eye-organ and the sensitive ear-organ, as explained above, until penetrative insight is fully attained.

Contemplation of Impact on the Sensitive Body Organ

The sensitive body-organ (*kāya-pasāda*) is spread in all flesh and blood tissues throughout the whole body system, from the top of the head to the soles of the feet. Any part of the body that senses pain when pricked with a sharp-pointed needle is impregnated with the sensitive body-organ. All kinds of sensation of hardness or softness belonging to the earth element group, of heat or cold belonging to the fire element group, or of the force of wind, whether strong or feeble, belonging to the wind element group, are bound to arrive at their destination of impact on the sensitive body-organ.

There is that part of the soles of the feet that experiences a sensation of heat when exposed to a furnace, or of coldness when bathed with water. Such sensations experienced by that part of the body are simultaneously reflected with a force of impact (1) on the sensitive body-organ located on the soles of the feet, and (2) on the mirrorlike element of the mind-base located within the heart. The force of such an impact is as tremendous as that of a striking thunderbolt. As an aftereffect of this force, the element of body-consciousness (*kāya-viññāṇa-dhātu*) arises all over the surface of the soles of the feet. At the same time the process of thought moments (*vīthi-citta*) of awareness of these sensations of heat or cold arise like a flowing current or stream. When such sensations of heat or cold disappear from the field of touch, the element of consciousness and the process of thought moments also disappear and die out.

It should be understood that the same is true of all parts of the body where the sensations of heat, cold, pain, shock, ache, weariness, numbness, congestion of internal organs, throbbing or pulsation are felt.

Here ends the exposition on the method of contemplating the point of conjunction of the three elements, namely: (1) the sensitive body-organ, (2) bodily-impression (phoṭṭhabbārammaṇa) and (3) body-consciousness, until penetrating insight is fully attained.

The Mirrorlike Element of the Mind-Base

The ceaseless arising of the subconscious "life continuum" (*bhavaṅga-citta*) which, like a mountain spring, always sparkles with a glitter of brilliant light within the heart, is called the mirrorlike element of the mind-base. This mirrorlike element of the mind-base, when not interrupted by a thought-process (*vīthi-citta*) adverts to the mind-object (*dhammārammaṇa*) pertaining to a former birth remembered there at the moment before death. Such adverting is, however, not a definite function (like that of a working consciousness) but only an indefinite one, and the object of this subconsciousness is not reflected in the consciousness of that individual. For there can be no such notion as, "I was subconsciously conscious of a certain mind-object during the dreamless period of my sleep throughout the whole night." When the mirrorlike element of the mind-base is flowing like the current of a river (without interruption by a process of thought or dream) the person concerned is as if in a state akin to death.

In cases where the image of a sense-object, such as that of the sun or moon, enters the range of vision, it acts on the sensitive eye-organ (*cakkhu-pasāda*), which is one of the five sense organs, and causes thereby a violent quivering in the subconscious stream (*bhavaṅga-sota*), just like the quivering occasioned when a snake or earthworm is disturbed with a staff or spear. However, as soon as the subconscious stream is broken, the functional mind-element, grasping the object, breaks through this subconscious stream and performs the function of cognizing the object in a process of conscious moments (*vīthi-citta*) arising like a series of flashes of a meteor or shooting stars in the sky.

In cases where the process of inner consciousness or mind consciousness takes place exclusively in the mind-base, that is, without the participation of the five physical sense consciousnesses of seeing, hearing, smelling, tasting, and bodily contact, the subconscious stream (*bhavaṅga-sota*) is broken off with a violent quivering in the same way as described above. Then there follow advertence (*āvajjana*) and impulsion (*javana*), which arise to perform their respective functions within the process of consciousness. When the force of impact of the sense object on the mind-element ceases, these functions of advertence and impulsion also die out and vanish just as the series of flashes of a meteor or shooting star fade out and vanish.

Here ends the exposition on the method of contemplating the point of conjunction of the three elements, namely: (1) the mirrorlike element of mind-base, called "subconsciousness" (bhavaṅga), (2) mind-object (dhammārammaṇa), and (3) mind-consciousness element (mano-viññāṇa-dhātu) until penetrating-insight is fully realized.

Here also ends the meaning of the description given in the second item of the matrix (mātikā) as: Its (i.e., the body's) whole interior is decorated with six kinds of clear and bright mirrorlike elements (chappasāda-maṇḍo).

Third Item of the Matrix

Thermal Conditions or Temperature

The third item is described as follows: "It (i.e., this body) is a product of ten kinds of thermal conditions or temperature (*ayaṃ kāyo utūnaṃ udayo*)."

The interpretation given in the scriptures of this term (*utu*) is "*Arati pavattatīti utu*" meaning "It has the characteristic of occurring endlessly."

The expanded interpretation of this term (*utu*) is "*Udati pasavatīti utu. Udanti pasavanti etena okāsa-satta-saṅkhāra-lokāti utu,*" meaning: "It is called temperature (*utu*). It is capable of generating growth and evolution. Due to this element an infinity of worlds classified as (a) the world of sentient beings (*satta-loka*), (b) the world of formations, or conditioned things (*saṅkhāra-loka*), and (c) the physical universe, or world of space (*okāsa-loka*), have been evolving in endless succession throughout the course of eternity."

The term *utu* in fact implies the element of fire, which is called *tejo-dhātu* as described earlier. It is this fire element that generates the growth and evolution in the endless succession of world systems throughout the course of eternity. It is this fire element that creates countless trillions of universes, or galaxies, each comprising countless billions of world systems. According to our theory, the Great Earth with its layers of rocks and dust (*silā-paṃsu*), measuring 240,000 *yojanas* in depth, rests on a mass of water measuring 480,000 *yojanas* in depth, which in turn rests on a mass of air measuring 960,000 *yojanas* in depth. The Great Earth in turn supports Mount Meru, the circumjacent mountains, the Himalaya mountains, the seven great lakes, the four great Oceans, the seven successive ranges of mountains around Mount Meru intervened by seven successive oceans of intense cold, the four great islands and the two thousand smaller ones. All these masses of land and water, including all masses of woodland and mountains and all planes of existence comprising the four lower worlds, the human world, the six heavenly abodes of deities, the twenty abodes of Brahmas rising up to the highest *Akaniṭṭhā* plane in the realms of form, whether belonging to a physical universe or to a world of space, are all the creative work of the fire element or element of heat and cold (*tejo-dhātu*).

The powers and potentialities of the element of heat and cold may be judged by a study of the *Satta Suriyopama Sutta* and *Aggañña Sutta* of the *Dīgha-Nikāya*, with the commentaries thereto, which give an account in detail of the destruction of an old world-cycle and the evolution of a new one.

Of the three cardinal elements of destruction i.e., fire, water and wind, the fire element means the element of heat, which is termed *uṇha-tejo*. When it is said that the Great Earth is destroyed by water, it does not mean that the destruction is wrought by water itself. It implies that the fire element as coldness (*sīta-tejo*), which is associated or synonymous with the water element (*āpo-dhātu*), is the actual destroyer. So the destruction wrought by the element of coldness should be regarded as being wrought by water. In the case of a world cycle destroyed by the wind element, it should be remembered that the element of heat (*uṇha-tejo*) is the principal generator of that wind element. So the main author of that great deluge or cataclysm is the fire element (*tejo-dhātu*). As an element that manifests, brings forth, generates what is ungenerated, develops that which is generated, the fire element is also the builder or creator of the universe.

Here ends the exposition on the building up of the physical universe, or the world of space (okāsa-loka).

The World of Sentient Beings

In the case of the world of sentient beings (*satta-loka*), one should judge the extent of the powers and potentialities of the fire element by making a study of the process of origination and the development of physical bodies of various sizes ranging from that of the minutest creature, which is normally invisible to the eye, to that of the gargantuan body of the great Brahmā in the highest plane of existence of the realm of form, called *Akaniṭṭhā.*

A study of the subject will reveal the fact that the primordial material units (*rūpa-kalāpa*) of sentient beings in the realm of form at the initial development phase (*ṭhiti*), the moment of their conception in a mother's womb, are conditioned by the volitional actions (*kamma*) performed by them during their past existences. It is the function of the fire element (*tejo-dhātu*) to promote, in due order, the origination, continuity, growth, and development of the material units from that initial development phase (*ṭhiti*) of the first moment of conception and to build up various physical organs of the body. The *kamma*-produced materiality (*kammaja-rūpa*), the mind-produced materiality (*cittaja-rūpa*), and the food-produced materiality (*āhāraja-rūpa*) arise sequentially following the development of physical organs of the body generated by the fire element. It is just like a lotus growth spreading out to all parts of a lake as far as the width of its surface permits.

The duration of life spans in the animal world, in the world of human beings, and of deities in the heavenly realms is also influenced and determined by this fire element. There are various grades of stability of the fire (heat or cold) element and various grades of subtlety of the physical bodies that form the physical base of this element. Long life spans are also on a graduated scale corresponding to these grades of stability and subtlety. And furthermore, there are various grades of instability of the fire element and grossness of the bodies that form the physical base of this element. Short life spans are on a graduated scale corresponding also to these same grades of instability and grossness.

In the case of womb-born sentient beings (*gabbha-seyyaka-satta*) the element of heat called "*utu,*" which is produced by the fertilization of an egg by sperm during sexual reproduction by both parents, is contributed as a hereditary factor of both father and mother. As the germinator of all material phenomena, the element of heat (*utu*) is the cosmic material generator of the birth (*jāti-niyāma-rūpa*) of sentient beings, just as it is the cosmic material germinator (*bīja-niyāma-rūpa*) of the vegetable kingdom, embracing plants, trees, etc. As a fixed (natural) order, the offspring inherits characteristics such as forms and features from its mother's or father's side. In the case of cross-breeding, such as between a serpent-king and a human-being or between a nymph and a human-being, it may be assumed that the acquired characteristics are inherited from the maternal or paternal side with a stronger nutritive essence in the physical body (*karaja-rūpa-ojā*).

Here ends the exposition on the building up of the world of sentient beings (satta-loka).

The World of Conditioned Things

The world of conditioned things in general (*saṅkhāra-loka*) embracing plants, trees, creepers, bushes, shrubs, etc., is solely a product of the element of heat. This fire element creates all kinds of plants, trees, creepers, bushes, and shrubs, together with all kinds of tubers, all kinds of sprouts, all kinds of shoots, all kinds of stems, all kinds of branches and twigs, all kinds of leaves, flowers, foliage, and fruits bearing various kinds of tastes, and sustains this generating and creating function until the end of the world. The creative work of the fire element is so marvellous that the world of fine arts showers praise on the sculptors who carve out figures and the artists who paint pictures of exact likeness to the picturesque leaves, fruits, and flowers created by the fire element. Just as sentient beings are governed by the cosmic law of birth (*jāti-niyāma*), conditioned things are governed by the cosmic law of germination (*bīja-niyāma*). All structural bodies of the universe, such as the sun, the moon, and heavenly bodies, such as the constellations and asteroids, and all treasures, such as gold, silver, pearls, and rubies, and all metals and chemicals, such as iron, brass, copper, and mercury, are the products of the fire element. Here ends the exposition on the building up of the world of conditioned things (*saṅkhāra-loka*).

Here ends the exposition on the building up of formations, or conditioned things (saṅkhāra-loka).

The Kinds of Fire Element

According to the declaration *udanti pasavanti etena okāsa satta saṅkhāra lokāti utu* this fire element is called *utu* because it is the cause of arising and propagation of the three worlds, namely,

1. The physical universe
2. The world of sentient beings
3. The world of conditioned things

and because it is the builder and creator of the three worlds of material phenomena.

This fire element is of two kinds, namely:

1. Internal fire element (*ajjhatta-tejo-dhātu*)
2. External fire element (*bahiddhā-tejo-dhātu*)

The former is divided into:

1. *Kamma* (volition) produced materiality (*kammaja-rūpa*)
2. Mind-produced materiality (*cittaja-rūpa*)
3. Materiality produced by temperature (*utuja-rūpa*)
4. Food-produced materiality (*āhāraja-rūpa*).

In terms of caste or class, grossness or subtleness, this fire element is of infinitely various kinds ranging from the bodily form of a denizen of the lowest purgatory (*avīci*) to that of the great Brahmā in the highest (*akaniṭṭhā*) plane of existence. The external fire element is briefly divided into:

1. Cold fire element (*sīta-tejo-dhātu*)
2. Hot fire element (*uṇha-tejo-dhātu*).

By way of caloric order (*utu-niyāma*) this fire element determines the ordered succession of the three seasons:

1. Hot season fire element (*gimha-tejo-dhātu*)
2. Rainy season fire element (*vassāna-tejo-dhātu*)
3. Cold season fire element (*hemanta-tejo-dhātu*).

By the same token what are called the "six *yatus*"[13] are, in fact, the six fire elements. Similarly, what are known as the twelve sub-seasons (*rāsī*) are but the twelve fire elements. Likewise, what are known as the one-hundred and eight "mystic number nine" actually represent the one-hundred and eight kinds of fire elements. Such entities as are known as the "eight planets" or "nine planets"—whose divinities are called Sunday Planet, Monday Planet, etc., are supposed to be riding on symbolic animals and occupying such cardinal points as Northeast, East, etc.—are also variations of the fire element. The ramifications of this element are so widely spread as to be found also in the terminology and nomenclature used in such branches of mundane arts and sciences as the Vedic scriptures (*veda*), pharmacology, metallurgic chemistry, astrology, and the cult of signs and omens.

In terms of class or caste, and of grossness or subtleness, this external fire element is of infinitely various kinds. The ten kinds of thermal conditions or temperature, as referred to in the third item of the matrix, is worked out as follows. When the four internal thermal conditions or fire elements, referred to above, are multiplied by the two elements of coldness (*sīta-tejo*) and heat (*uṇha-tejo*), we get a resultant figure of eight internal fire elements. The external fire element is of two kinds only, namely, the cold external fire element and the hot external element. When the two groups are added together they make a total of ten kinds of fire element.

Burning and Vanishing

All kinds of material phenomena, whether animate or inanimate, consist merely of groups or collections of fire element. This element of heat and cold is in a state of perpetual burning, or combustion, and as such the groups and collections of material phenomena are forever blazing away into radiation in a seething turmoil. You should contemplate with clear comprehension and penetrating insight these phenomena occurring in your brain cells, eyeballs, and other regions of your body right down to the soles of your feet. Within the framework of such combustion in a seething turmoil, there is an uninterrupted process of building up of new material units in all parts of your body. This building up is momentarily followed by a breaking down process of burning up and vanishing. This arising and dissolution process in the body appears, to those who feel it, as a series of minute eruptions or vibrations.

Ultimate Realities

In the realm of ultimate realities (*paramattha-dhamma*), there is no phenomenon of motion or shakiness that is visible to the physical eye. With the phenomena of new entities arising in a series intertwined with the dissolution of old entities in a series, there is bound to be created in an observer the common sense idea of movement of the same (identical) thing. This gives rise to such notions as "rising," "getting-up," "falling-down," "going," and "coming." Only an observer who, with penetrative insight, dissects and discerns these phenomena, can dispel such false notions. When such insight knowledge is in the early stage of development, the aforesaid common-sense ideas are likely to obstruct and interfere with realising the truth that is hidden behind appearances. When such notions interfere with the practice of insight-contemplation of the elements of the body in the ultimate sense, penetration into ultimate realities is likely to be retarded through the intervention of pictorial ideas or concepts of collectivity and form (*samūha-saṇṭhāna-paññatti*) and the concept of continuity (*santati-paññatti*).

Samūha-saṇṭhāna-paññatti is a term implying shape and mass. When a contemplative knowledge is interfered with by the concept of shape and mass it cannot gain penetration into ultimate realities.

The Concept of Continuity

Except for *Nibbāna* there is no phenomenon in the realm of ultimate reality (*paramattha-dhamma*) that can abide for even the wink of an eye. All other phenomena are mere processes of arising and dissolution. When two different phenomena—one of dissolution and another of arising—are mixed up in a series of rapid succession, the old (preceding) phenomenon that has dissolved and the newly arisen (succeeding) phenomenon appear to be one and the same phenomenon. This delusive appearance to the mind (of common sense thinking) is called the concept of continuity (*santati-paññatti*). When this concept interferes with insight knowledge, the mind is deluded into thinking that one and the same (identical) thing has "happened like this," "happened like that," "reached here," "reached there," "has moved," "has arisen," "has stood-up," etc. One should, therefore, contemplate with penetrative insight and discernment the difference between the concept of collectivity (*samūha-paññatti*), the concept of the form of things (*saṇṭhāna-paññatti*), and the concept of the continuity of things on the one hand, and the ultimate realities on the other hand. These are the groups of words describing the deceptions practised by concepts with regard to such appearances as shaking, quaking, quivering, and trembling. In the section dealing with the fire element we have, to some extent, described the powers and potentialities of this fire element that is referred to in various texts as "temperature" or "heat" (*utu*). If what has been described in that section, in conjunction with what has been briefly described above, is fully grasped, one will be able to realize with penetrative insight the tremendous and marvellous omnipotence of this fire element, and its predominance in all three worlds described above, which are but mere products of the fire element.

Here ends the exposition of the meaning of the expression "This body is a product of ten kinds of thermal conditions or temperature," made in the third item of the matrix.

Fourth Item of the Matrix

The Ten Kinds of Nutriment

In the fourth item this passage occurs: "This physical body is perpetually supported by the ten kinds of nutriment (*ayaṃ kāyo thambhito āhārehi*)." What has been referred to above and in other texts as nutrient essence (*ojā*) or nutriment (*āhāra*) means the ultimate physical essence, which is also called "essence element." In two interpretations in the texts, it is called nutrient essence and nutriment (*āhāra*) as follows: "It is called nutrient essence because it produces material phenomena in the immediately following instant *udayānantaraṃ rūpaṃ janetīti ojā*)." It is called nutriment (*āhāra*) because it greatly supports and produces the eightfold material phenomena having nutrient essence as its eighth factor, i.e., the solid, liquid, heat, motion, colour, odour, the tastable, and the nutrient essence (*ojaṭṭhamakaṃ rūpaṃ āhāratīti āhāro*).

The Two Kinds of Essence

The essence element is of two kinds, namely:

1. Interior essence element
2. Exterior essence element.

Just as the fire element (*tejo-dhātu*) is of ten kinds, eight internal and two external, the corresponding essence element is also of ten kinds. The functions of this essence element include causing the arising of food-produced material units (*āhāraja-rūpa-kalāpa*) and supporting the four causes for the arising of the material phenomena of sentient beings of the sensuous world (*catu-rūpa-samuṭṭhānika*). By the expression, "the function of causing the arising of food-produced material units," is meant the production of two kinds of substances, namely fat (*medo*) and skin grease (*vasā*). The material phenomena of sentient beings of the sensuous world cannot subsist even for a period occupied by the wink of an eye without material food (*āhāra*). For this reason the question of earning a living is a problem of the greatest magnitude in the world. If one can see the land creatures and water denizens everywhere in the world that are incessantly toiling and struggling to eke out a living, day and night, throughout their whole lifetime, one will be able to judge the magnitude of the problem of earning a living. If one can see the extent and magnitude of the problem of earning a living, one will be able to size up the problem of acquiring food. If one can size up the problem of acquiring food, one will be able to appreciate the magnitude of the function of support carried out by the essence element and the inability of the internal material phenomena to survive even for a period occupied by the wink of an eye without the support of the external essence element.

The Simile of the Rainbow

The following example may be given to illustrate the point. In this physical body there are four constituent elements, namely:

1. The quality of hardness or softness called the earth element (*paṭhavī-dhātu*)
2. The quality of cohesiveness or liquidity, called the water element (*āpo-dhātu*)
3. The quality of heat or cold, called the fire element (*tejo-dhātu*)
4. The quality of strong support or weak support, called the wind element (*vāyo-dhātu*).

We would ask you to remember what we have said before, that they are like the image of a man reflected in a mirror, or like images of the sun, moon, clouds, or the sky above, reflected on the surface of placid waters and to keep this in your mind. There is in the sky that which is called by various names such as "rainbow," "the colossal wedge," "the plough-handle," or "god-king's loincloth."

This rainbow shows up just outside the rain clouds in the western sky if the rays of the sun coming from the eastern sky reflect on the moisture-saturated atmosphere. If the sun's rays come from the west and the rain clouds are occupying the eastern sky, the rainbow shows up on the outside of rain clouds on the east. As the sun is the originating factor of a rainbow, the disappearance of the sun means the disappearance of the rainbow also. As it also depends on the rain clouds for its arising, the disappearance of the rain clouds also means the disappearance of the rainbow. The sun constitutes a contributory factor by causing the form of the rainbow to arise, while the rain clouds constitute another contributory factor by supporting such a formation with a basis. In whatever portion of the sky the sun's rays are absent, in that portion the rainbow also disappears or shows its form partly cut out. If the sun's rays totally disappear, the rainbow also totally disappears. In whatever part of the sky the rain clouds are absent, in that part also the rainbow disappears or shows its form partly cut out. Whenever the rain clouds are thin, the rainbow shows up with a faint appearance. When the rain clouds with their supporting basis disappear, the rainbow also disappears instantaneously even though the sun's rays are present on that spot.

In this simile the moral and immoral actions committed in previous existences (*kamma*) resemble the sun in the sky, while the volition-produced fire element (*kammaja-tejo-dhātu*) and its associates, the mind-produced fire element (*cittaja-tejo-dhātu*), the temperature-produced fire element (*utuja-tejo-dhātu*), and the food-produced fire element (*āhāraja-tejo-dhātu*), resemble the rays of the sun. The essence element, which is steeped in all parts of the body, resembles the mass of the rain cloud. The four great primary elements (*mahā-bhūta*) of the body resemble the great form of the rainbow. When it is said that the essence element resembles the rain cloud, it means resemblance in the function of giving support. When the result of past *kamma* and the volition-produced fire element become spent, the four great primary elements (*mahā-bhūta*) of the body also become destroyed and lost although the essence element is still subsisting. Even when the result of the past *kamma* is still persisting, if the external essence element becomes totally spent due to lack of food, the internal essence element will be devoid of strength and the mass of the four great primary elements (*mahā-*

bhūta) is bound to perish. Let the example of the rainbow cited above be fully applied to this case and studied in conjunction for better understanding.

In the item dealing with the four great primary elements we have given the example of the images reflected in a mirror or on the surface of placid waters. In that simile, the moral and immoral actions performed in previous existences (*kamma*) and the group of fire elements (*tejo-dhātu*) resemble the man's face, sun, moon, and clouds. The essence element group resembles the mirror and the surface of the waters. The four great primary elements of the body resemble the image of the man's face, and the images of the sun, moon, and the great cloud bank. In this example also, the resemblance is in respect only of the function of support or bracing-up. With these examples we have shown how this body of ours, which is composed of the four great primary elements and the six sense bases, is subsisting with the support and bracing-up of the external essence element, and how, without such support and bracing-up, it is bound to perish.

The Oil Essence Element

We now propose to deal with the manner of support or bracing-up. In this world it is an obvious fact that oil and fire are complementary to each other. All kinds of oil are developed only by association with fire, and fire is developed and made to subsist only by association with oil. All kinds of oil, including crude oil and kerosene oil, which are called "earth oil," and sesame oil, linseed oil, groundnut oil, and oil produced by animals, such as butter or ghee, tend to produce fire that thrives on such oils. These are statements of obvious facts in regard to oils that are evident. The material essence, called "nutrient essence" is inherent in all kinds of material units. Even various objects are endowed with the oil-essence element. In the case of the burning of a loincloth, hay, dried leaves, firewood or wood-stuff, it is in fact the oil-essence element that is the food actually consumed by the fire. As fire develops in proportion to the volume of available oil-essence, it burns up and consumes all material phenomena with which the oil-essence element is coexistent. This fact should be carefully observed until it is fully realized.

The Earth Oil Simile

In medieval Burma, dramatic shows were acted not on a stage but on the ground in an open space surrounding a rose apple tree (*Eugenia*). For night performances the place was lit up with a flaming torch on a pole or pillar planted in the middle of the open space. The torch, in the middle, was a huge pot fitted with a wick. Earth oil was fed into that pot and the wick was ignited. The life of the flame thus produced depended on the earth oil fed into that pot. If the volume of the earth oil thus fed was big, the strength of the flame grew big. If the quantity of earth oil fed into the pot was small, the strength of the flame grew weak. When that fuel oil was used up, the flame disappeared. In this simile the three great primary elements, namely, the earth element, the water element, and the wind element, together with the six sense bases, resemble the flaming torch on the pillar. The internal oil-essence element, which is steeped in all parts of the body, resembles the earth oil already existing in the (oil-container of the) flaming torch pillar. The fire element in all parts of the body resembles the flames burning both inside and outside the flaming-torch-pillar. The external oil-essence element (nutriment-essence) contained in the food consumed daily by sentient beings resembles the earth oil that has to be fed into the flaming torch intermittently and without end. In the preceding section, we have given the example of a rainbow in the sky in order to stress the magnitude of the task of supplying the oil-essence element. In the present section we have cited the example of a flaming-torch-pillar to illustrate the function of the oil-essence in giving rise to physical units and maintaining them with supplies and support.

To further elucidate: the food that is swallowed down into the stomach is composed of eight units only, having nutrient essence as its eighth factor. So every unit contains the oil-essence element that supports the four great primaries. It should, therefore, be said, figuratively, that if the edible food measures a cubic-foot, the constituent nutrient essence also measures a cubic-foot. Just as strong pillars and posts prop up and buttress an old house built on piles that are rotting away in the ground, the nutrient essence, contained in the newly swallowed food, gives strength and vitality to the internal material units of the whole body as soon as the food reaches the stomach. Just as weak props and weak buttresses make an old house shake and sway, because the collapse of such props and buttresses leads to the collapse of the old house, even so, the six-hour-old material units, together with their internal constituent essence element, gradually disintegrate and totally vanish. It is because the newly consumed food remains fresh as an energy supplier for just six or seven hours, beyond which it begins to decompose and disintegrate. When the life-term of the latest food in the stomach expires, all energy-supplying elements in the body dissolve leaving only the temperature-produced group of gross elements called "waste products" or "carcass" (*mata-kalevara*).

The Weakening of Bodily Strength

Meals are taken once or twice a day before the last consumed food in the stomach becomes completely exhausted. People know well that their strength weakens when hunger sets in. They are pathetically ignorant of the fact that from the moment the food supply in the stomach begins to drain off, the internal material groups, element groups, unitary groups, vitality groups, and energy groups are gradually wearing out and dissolving away. Just as the rainbow, in the simile mentioned above, dissolves when its support basis, the rain cloud, dissolves, there is a gradual wearing away and disintegration in the whole body of the great mass, called the quality of hardness (*paṭhavī-dhātu*), the quality of cohesiveness called the water element, the quality of heat or coldness called the fire element, and the quality of stiffness or tension called the wind element. In the same instance there is also a gradual wearing away and dissolution of the sensitive eye-organ (*cakkhu-pasāda*), the sensitive ear-organ, the sensitive nose-organ, the sensitive tongue-organ, the sensitive body-organ, the mind-base or consciousness (*manāyatana*), and the clusters of subtle elements and material units inside the head, inside the chest, inside the abdomen, inside the hips, inside the thighs, inside the legs, and inside the soles of the feet. They are just like mass dissolutions of water bubbles of huge froths and foams in a series of ceaseless turmoil. These processes of dissolution should be carefully observed and contemplated until they are vividly seen with the eye of wisdom. Just as the weakening of props and buttresses means the swaying and collapsing of the dilapidated house built on piles in the ground, even so the clusters of subtle material units and elements inside the body will be swaying and collapsing if the energy-supplying food inside the stomach is exhausted. This fact also should be carefully observed and contemplated until it is fully realized.

When it is said that bodily strength is weakened due to hunger, it means the collapse and disintegration of lumps of material units and elements called "energy," just like falling snowflakes. A person oppressed with hunger is conspicuous by the depressed and worn-out look of his face and eyes. By seeing the depressed look of the exterior, it can be inferred that the lumps of internal materiality, elements, and units have been collapsing and disintegrating so heavily that the remaining elements are greatly reduced in strength. The change in gradual stages of the quality of hardness means, in terms of ultimate realities (*paramattha-dhamma*), the gradual dissolution of the earth element. In such terms, the change in gradual stages of the quality of cohesiveness means the gradual dissolution of the water element. The same is true of the dissolution of the other two elements (*tejo* and *vāyo*).

Here ends the exposition on the exhaustion and dissolution of elements.

How the Oil-Essence Element is Supplied to the Whole Body

When exhaustion begins, new food has to be swallowed before the old supply of food is completely exhausted. As soon as the swallowed food reposes in the stomach, the four great primary elements become revitalised instantaneously, just as a leaning structure is levelled and propped up with posts and pillars, masses of strength, energy, and vitality then become fully restored. The fact is made evident by external looks and appearances. If the interior organs are given a penetrating look (with insight), one may be able to see them filling instantaneously with material units, just as heavy rain makes hollows, depressions, lakebeds, stream beds, and drains fill with water.

The main intestine (stomach), which is called the receptacle for new food, resembles a very loose and coarse loincloth, canvas or sackcloth. Under this receptacle a cooking apparatus or firebox (*pācaka*) is located. The converging point of tendons, which is commonly known in Burmese as "*takyee,*" is called the cooking fire-box. In this firebox is located the volition-produced *kamma* (*kammaja*) fire element, called "cooking" (*pācaka*) fire. Another *kamma*-produced fire element, called "the original bodily-warmth" (*usmā*), that protects and vitalizes the whole body is also a product of the "cooking-fire" element. This element performs the task of cooking the newly eaten food that reaches the stomach. It is just like cooking cow's milk or goat's milk in manufacturing butter or ghee. In this cooking process four kinds of product are turned out. They are fine and coarse solids and fine and coarse liquids. The coarse solids and liquids, which are deficient in nutrient essence (*ojā*), gravitate downward, while the nutrient-rich essence and oils rise upward. This way of cooking newly eaten food, and separating it into fine or coarse qualities of solids and liquids, is called "the process of cooking by stomach (gastric) fire."

The coarse solids turn into faeces or excreta and gravitate into the receptacle for "old food" (i.e., the intestines). The coarse liquids turn into urine and gravitate into the urinary bladder. All nutrient oil-essence boiled by the "cooking-fire" element and by the "bodily-warmth" element (*usmā*) boils over and spreads throughout the whole body along the one-thousand "taste-conductor nerves" (*rasa-haraṇī*). During the circulation process the nutrient oil-essence comes in contact with the fire element located in all parts of the body. When this happens, the oil element tends in this world to promote growth and development of the nutrient-essence, whether heated by fire or not. And when it becomes associated with bodily-warmth fire elements, it multiplies the growth of material units (*rūpa-kalāpa*). In addition, it promotes the growth of fat and skin grease. When associated with the oil-essence element, the fire element throughout the whole body tends to flare up and develop just as ordinary fires flare up when fed with oil or fat. In the world of trade or manufacture, oil or essence is extracted from various objects by the process of heating with fire. In such undertakings, if the strength of fire (heat) is weak, less essence and more waste matter is produced. Similarly, if the stomach-fire, which is called digestive (cooking) fire (*pācaka-tejo*) is weak, all the food that is eaten and swallowed into the stomach will be reduced more into waste products, such as faeces, urine, wind, and phlegm, and less into oil-essence, which is referred to in nutritional science books as "taste element" (*rasa-dhātu*).

If, on the other hand, the heat of the digestive fire is excessive, all the food eaten and swallowed into the stomach is generally burnt up leaving only a small quantity of oil-essence element as residue. If the fire element is enmeshed or overlaid with wind and phlegm, the smothered heat will be so weak and unbalanced that the food will not be properly digested. When nutrition is thus impaired, the power of resistance will be weakened and the physical body will be susceptible to all forms of diseases. Ordinary food, by itself, is not fully endowed with nutrient-essence (*ojā*) and, as already described in the section relating to the second attribute of a person making the supreme effort (*padhāniyaṅga*), people of the present time are prone to fall sick easily and also to die easily. This is due to the turbulent and unbalanced state of the two fires known as the digestive-fire and the bodily-warmth fire. We have also described how it was possible for some people to secure for themselves immunity from the danger of diseases and extend their life spans, beyond the normal life span of a century, to two-hundred, three-hundred, four-hundred, five-hundred, nay, a thousand years. It was achieved by imbibing the tonics or elixirs that were prepared by transmuting an essence-element, bearing metals such as iron or mercury, into other forms. Because such tonics or elixirs blend well and are compatible with the delicate internal elements, those twin fires are rendered docile. Thus marvellous results as described above are produced.

Here ends the interpretation of the expression contained in the fourth item (mātikā): This physical body is perpetually supported by the ten kinds of nutriment.

Fifth Item of the Matrix

The Process of Primary Origination

We shall now explain the significance of the expression: "This body has the characteristic of origination in an uninterrupted process" (*ayaṃ kāyo jātidhammo*). Earlier we have given the example of images reflected in a mirror and the example of a rainbow in the sky. We have also described the function of the digesting fire element in the process of preparing the oil-essence element together with the various problems involved therein. If all the facts and events so described are carefully observed and studied, it will become evident with regard to the body that there is no respite, even for the period occupied by the wink of an eye or a flash of lightning, in the successive arising of new phenomena, nor the successive dissolution of old phenomena. It will also become evident that just on account of the fire element and the oil-essence element, there is a continuous bustle and confusion of arisings and dissolvings just like the seething turmoil of churning waters in a boiling cauldron. The quality of hardness or the earth element (*paṭhavī-dhātu*) arises in all parts of the body. It is conditioned by four factors, namely:

1. Wholesome or unwholesome actions of the past (*kamma*)
2. Consciousness (*citta*)
3. Temperature (*utu*)
4. Nutriment (*āhāra*)

This element is devoid of any substance even to the extent of an atom, and is merely a quality or characteristic. This hardness is, therefore, instantly destroyed due to the energy of the fire element, because it cannot continue to exist even for a period occupied by the wink of an eye. When it is so destroyed its coexistent elements of cohesiveness, heat or coldness, and stiffness or tension also have to join in this total dissolution. Likewise, the six sensitive organs depending on that earth element have to join in. This fact should be observed in all parts of the body.

All places vacated by the dissolved elements are also filled by replacements of the same kind. In this manner, there is an uninterrupted change of coming into being and passing away with a frequency of more than a hundred or a thousand times within a period occupied by a wink of an eye or a flash of lightning. These arisings and dissolvings are not visible to the eye. They can be seen only with the eye of wisdom by drawing inferences from the observable phenomena. All manifestations of shaking or trembling imply the dissolution of the old and its replacement by the arising of new phenomena. To the observing eye, however, it has the appearance of one and the same (identical) visual object, shaking or moving. When conventional sense perception is regarded as truth or reality, a penetrative insight into ultimate realities (*paramattha-dhamma*) becomes an impossible proposition. One should ponder this point well and exercise the utmost care.

The Consuming Nature of the Fire Element

We have said a while ago that such ultimate realities as the earth element and the water element, which are conditioned by the four factors of *kamma, citta, utu,* and *āhāra,* are instantly destroyed by the coexistent fire element. We should like to explain in this respect that fires, by nature, have the trait of burning up the objects that are the basis of their origination. In accordance with this nature, the fire element of the ultimate sphere burns up into nothingness in a succession of moments, as do the other three coexistent elements called "hardness," "cohesiveness" and "tenseness," together with the six sense bases. The fire that originates from waste matter eats up all waste matter in a short moment. The fire that originates from oil similarly eats up all oil. The fire that originates from earth oil eats up all earth oil in a short moment. The fire that originates in a particular kind of fat or grease eats up all such fat or grease in a short moment.

Likewise, the fire element that is ever burning in all parts of each body of sentient beings eats up all coexistent elements in a succession of moments. In particular, all oil elements are completely eaten up in a short moment.

Such being the case, all kinds of elements, such as the earth element or the water element belonging to the ultimate sphere cannot exist or remain alive even for the period occupied by the wink of an eye or a flash of lightning. They all vanish completely inside the whole body with a frequency of more than a hundred or a thousand times during the time occupied by the wink of an eye. In spite of the speed of such an evanescent process, there is so large a number of conditioning factors, and all elements that have vanished are so fully replaced and renewed, that persons of a young age are able to grow up and develop (in strength) from moment to moment. One should contemplate the process of dissolution that is going on without respite all over one's own body until it is fully realized. If one can grasp the process of dissolution in shorter phases of minute detail, one will be able to grasp the process of replacements and renewals going on all over one's own body that are taking place in events of origination in similarly shorter phases of minute detail. A fire that originates in a barrel of kerosene oil will keep on burning briskly until the whole quantity is exhausted.

But if someone keeps on replenishing the diminished oil, neither the quantity of kerosene oil nor the light of the fire will appear to have diminished. Contrary to such appearance, the fact remains that both kerosene oil and the fire element are dissolving away in momentary phases.

The Difficulty in Maintaining the Body-Mind Process

Were there no dissolution process, there would be no necessity for replenishing with new oil. If fifty barrels of kerosene oil were used in repeatedly replenishing throughout the whole night, it is evident that fifty barrels of kerosene oil were consumed by the fire. By intently watching and carefully studying this, it will be seen that both the kerosene oil and the corresponding fire are dissolving away from moment to moment. The gradual diminishing in quantity of kerosene oil and fire can also be observed. People also know that a large quantity of kerosene oil is consumed in lighting for one night. One should calculate just how many hours one's body can remain in full zest and vigour after partaking of a meal. One should take notice that in proportion to the reduction of food, one's body is reduced in strength and vigour. One should therefore deduce that one's body will exist no more if the stomach is empty. Because the frequency of dissolution of component elements of this body is tremendous, the frequency of replacements and replenishings is also tremendous. And because the pace of maintaining the continuity of this breaking-down-and-building-up process is so tremendous, earning of a living in this world is a task of the greatest magnitude, utmost difficulty, supreme inescapability, and an absolute necessity.

If one can imagine the massive quantity of food crops, such as paddy, beans, maize, millet, and all kinds of cereals, pulses, legumes, and nuts, grown and harvested each year throughout the whole island continent of rose apple trees (*jambudīpa*), and the yearly, monthly or daily rate of consumption of these foodstuffs, one would appreciate the magnitude of the task of renewal and the ongoing concern for the maintenance and continuance of the five aggregates. If the magnitude and difficulty of the never-ending task of renewal and maintenance of the five aggregates, i.e., of earning a living, is realized, the tremendous speed at which mental and physical phenomena are dissolving and vanishing in succession will also be appreciated. If one can investigate fully from its source the animated scene of all sentient beings, including water denizens and land-creatures, outstripping each other in fetching, carrying, transporting, coming, going, discussing, negotiating, planning, exercising restless care, ceaselessly striving, anxiously worrying, watching, tending, arguing, and quarrelling, for the sake of a livelihood, for food and economic necessities, one will realize that it is all due to the difficulty of ensuring continuity by bridging the immediately preceding body and life with the immediately succeeding body and life.

If the difficulty of ensuring continuity by renewal and replacement is envisaged, the tremendous speed with which the old phenomena are dissolving and vanishing, and the fact that they are devoid of a core or essence, will be realized. By all these expressions we mean to drive home the point that infinite worries and anxieties are arising in this world just because of the tremendous rate at which the component elements, big or small, of the mind-body complex are arising and vanishing in an uninterrupted process. These are the pointers to primary origination (*pakati-jāti*).

Because of attachment to the five aggregates (*khandha*), there arises the aspiration to live a longer life, say a hundred or a thousand years. To achieve this purpose, continuity is devised by bridging the succession of new, instantly-arising originations by means of earning a living, which is called "maintenance." By such means, an uninterrupted process of arisings or new originations is maintained. If one clearly comprehends the process of primary origination, one will also clearly comprehend the process of changing origination (*vikati-jāti*).

The Principle of Changed Origination

"Changing origination" (*vikati-jāti*) means the arising of various sores, the arising of various diseases, the arising of various dangers, the arising of various enmities, the arising of various punishments, and the arising of various accidents. Because there is an ever-recurring process of origination, which links and joins up the old with the new without a break or interruption in continuity or flow, the changeover from pleasantness to unpleasantness can take place in a fleeting moment. Also because the process of dissolution is running at a tremendous frequency, the changeover from pleasantness to unpleasantness, or from happiness to misery, can take place in a fleeting moment. There is no fleeting moment at which the origination of unpleasantness or misery cannot take place.

The Similes of the Snake Venom and the Gunpowder-Packed Rocket

The Pāḷi term *jāti* means "arising," "origination," or "genesis." In the expression "eye-sore arises" and "ear-ache arises" the word "arises" signifies origination or genesis. Both internally and externally, the factors for the origination of unpleasantness and misery are infinitely numerous. Hence the Blessed One has allegorized the quality of hardness or earth element, which is the main basis of the five aggregates (*khandha*), as a snake of the *kaṭṭhamukha* species. If a person is bitten by such a snake at the tip of his toe, the snake venom speedily spreads right up to his head and he falls into a fainting fit. The whole body changes both in colour and composition. The original material units of the whole body vanish and a new materiality group resembling a body electrocuted by a lightning strike becomes instantaneously established. Nothing, not even an atom of the original body remains, and the whole body is entirely filled with new material units resembling the components of a body electrocuted by a lightning strike.

Suppose there is a rocket fully charged with fifty barrels of highly explosive gun powder. If a spark were to gain access into the gun powder chamber of that rocket through a fuse-conduit hole, the fifty barrels of gun powder would catch fire all at once.

You might like to know how the whole body of the snake-bitten person in the above mentioned simile is transformed into a new body and how the original body disappeared. It is to be explained in this way. As everyone knows, the original body standing firmly on the soles of the feet (before the snakebite) is a materiality group in perfect harmony and pleasantness. When bitten by the snake, however, the snake venom spreads all over the body reaching up to the head. This causes unhappiness and disharmony due to feelings and sensations of inflammation, acute pain, constriction, cramp, being prodded or sandbagged, sluggishness, stiffness, and strained tensions. All these feelings and sensations were originally absent, but becoming manifest now, they give rise to disharmony and unpleasantness. If asked, the snake-bitten person will surely reply that there occurred in that moment a transformation. Such a reply would be pathetically ignorant of the truth in the ultimate sense, in that it is in fact a newly originated body composed entirely of new material units and elements.

What is commonly believed to be the self-same or identical body, undergoing such and such vicissitudes and being afflicted by such and such a disease or ailment, is indeed a succession of new originations, new materialities, new elements, new units, and new ultimate realities. When one feels hot in a certain part, or throughout the whole of one's body, one should know that it is a new origination that has taken place in that moment. When a new body arises, the old body is bound to disappear. When one feels with discernment that one's body is now growing hot, one understands that the old materiality group, element group, and material-unit group have disappeared. The change is so instantaneous that it is impossible to notice it.

Whenever one experiences such disagreeable feelings as cold, pain, numbness, ache, stress, stiffness, tenseness, stricture, cramp, itch, strain, or heat, one should bear in mind that in the part of the body where such feelings arise the old materiality has disappeared and a new origination with new materiality has been substituted. During attacks of fever characterized by shivering cold, the rising or subsiding of cold or heat, as the case may be, are clear indications of substitution or replacement of the old materiality with an entirely new one. There are infinite varieties of disagreeable experiences sustained by this body, such as a sudden onset of illness due to partaking food to which one is allergic, or bathing at the wrong time, or being drenched by rain. These are the words with which the various kinds of changing origination (*vikati-jāti*) are described.

Fear and Worries due to Change

Due to the obvious existence of this principle of changing origination, people are in constant dread, fear, and fright. They are tormented by worries and anxieties over all kinds of possible dangers, enmities, punishments, and accidents, both internal and external to the body. They have to exercise restraint in their staying, going, coming, doing, and behaving just as they wish.

They have to lead restricted and circumscribed lives by living in organized communities of villages or towns, and in houses with compounds and protective barriers, in order to avoid such dangers. If such narrow and difficult ways of living are observed, one would be able to see the principle of changing origination as the reason for such restricted ways of living.

Here ends the exposition on the tremendous frequency with which the quality of hardness, or earth element, which is the fundamental basis of the whole and which is allegorized by the Buddha as a snake of the kaṭṭhamukha species, arises and vanishes in a process. As an aid to that exposition the examples of a snake-bitten person and a gun powder-packed rocket have been given.

The Simile of the Lump of Wax

Let us take the case of a very hard lump of sealing wax or candle wax or fat the size of a man, which is heated by fire, whose radiation reaches both the outside and inside of the lump. You should watch and carefully note the fact that when it is affected by the heat of fire, the quality of hardness disintegrates by gradual stages and the quality of softness increases by gradual stages. When the fire is withdrawn and kept away from the wax, you should also note carefully that the quality of softness disintegrates by gradual stages and the quality of hardness increases by gradual stages. In the Discourses of the Sutta Piṭaka, and in the Higher Teaching (Abhidhamma Piṭaka), the expression "disintegration by gradual stages" is represented in different terms such as "extinction" (*nirodha*), "passing away" (*bhaṅga*), "dissolution" (*khaya*), "vanishing" (*vaya*), "disappearance" (*attha*), "death" (*maraṇa*), and "impermanence" (*anicca*).

The Higher Knowledge of the Truth of Impermanence

Insight trainees (*vipassanā-yogī*) must contemplate such phenomena until an objective knowledge of "impermanence" is attained. Such knowledge is called "the higher knowledge of the truth of impermanence" (*anicca-vijjā-ñāṇa*). If the origination of the earth element, which has been allegorized as a snake of the *kaṭṭhamukha* species, is fully comprehended, the disintegration and arising ever anew in a continuous process of the other coexisting primary elements will also be comprehended. The coexisting primary elements are: 1. the water element, which has been allegorized as a snake of the *pūtimukha* species; 2. the fire element, which has been allegorized as a snake of *aggimukha* species; 3. the wind element, which has been allegorized as a snake of *sattamukha* species.

The increase or disintegration by gradual stages of the quality of cohesiveness in the water element is, indeed, a gradual extinction, passing away, dissolution, vanishing, disappearance, death, and impermanence.

The increase or disintegration by gradual stages of the quality of heat in the fire element is, indeed, a gradual extinction, passing away, dissolution, vanishing, disappearance, death, and impermanence.

The increase or disintegration by gradual stages of the quality of tension or stiffness in the wind element is, indeed, a gradual extinction, passing away, dissolution, vanishing, disappearance, death, and impermanence.

Only this kind of comprehension of "impermanence" qualifies as genuine insight knowledge (*vipassanā-ñāṇa*). The mere intellectual knowledge or contemplation of the idea of (anthropomorphic) death of individuals in the course of time as a necessary consequence of the process of living is definitely not an insight knowledge. Worldlings of all classes, castes, and races know this (anthropomorphic) kind of death. The same remarks apply equally to the idea of old age and disintegration.

If the sign of impermanence (*aniccā-lakkhaṇa*) in the arising and dissolving process of the four great primaries is observed with insight, no special effort needs to be made to comprehend the six sense bases together with the fire element and nutrient essence (oil) element. Such comprehension is bound to be achieved automatically.

Here ends the interpretation of the expression contained in the fifth item of the matrix: This body has the characteristic of origination in an uninterrupted process.

Sixth Item of the Matrix

The Process of Momentary Decay

We shall now explain the significance of the expression: "This body has the characteristic of decaying momentarily in a process" (*ayaṃ kāyo jarādhammo*) contained in the sixth item of the matrix.

If one has comprehended all that we have said with regard to origination (*jāti*), and particularly to the point that there is no phenomenon even to the extent of an atom that can endure for a period occupied by the wink of an eye or a flash of lightning, one will also be able to comprehend the idea of decay. In this world there is no case of dissolution that is not preceded by decay and disintegration. All objects tending to become dissolved have to move from a state of cheerful brightness and newness to one of decrease and decay.

It is a matter of intelligent observation that in the sphere of ultimate realities, dissolutions are always preceded by decrease and decay, becoming worn out, putrid, or rotten. This fact should be quite obvious.

Here ends the exposition on the phenomenon of decay.

Seventh Item of the Matrix

The Process of Momentary Death

We propose next to explain the significance of the expression: "This physical body has the characteristic of momentarily dying in a process" (*ayaṃ kāyo maraṇadhammo*). In previous chapters we have mentioned the following terms: extinction (*nirodha*), dissolution (*bhaṅga*), passing-away (*khaya*), vanishing (*vaya*), disappearance (*attha*), death (*maraṇa*), and impermanence (*anicca*). They all bear the same connotation as the term "death" insofar as ultimate realities (*paramattha-dhamma*) are concerned. The term "death" means momentary dissolutions and vanishings because of the disaster of being consumed by the fires of the primary elements and decay. For as we have said earlier, the constituents of the body are without an essence or core and are incapable of abiding even for a period occupied by the wink of an eye or a flash of lightning.

"Death" (in this context) means the dissolution and vanishing of the whole body, complete and entire, in a disastrous process occurring more than a hundred times during the wink of an eye or a flash of lightning. For example, let us imagine that a very fresh and sprightly lotus is plucked away from its water habitat in a pond and placed on the land, high and dry. This lotus is assailed by three adversities, namely:

1. Perceptible decay (*santati-jarā*)
2. Decay in momentary phases (*khaṇika-jarā*)
3. Death in momentary phases (*khaṇika-maraṇa*)

It therefore withers and perishes. In this instance the conspicuous "perceptible decay" arises due to the following contributory factors:

1. Being deprived of the support of water that is its life principle,
2. Being subjected to the onset of the element of heat generated by the sun's rays, by the scorched earth, and by the heated water

"Perceptible decay" means the decrease, depreciation, shrinkage, and withering away that is obvious to the eye. The fact is plain through mere sight. The final dissolution on coming to an end is also perceptible to the eye. When perceptible decay is seen with the eye, "decay" in momentary phases and "death" in momentary phases will become clearly perceptible to the eye of wisdom. Of course, these two latter phenomena are invisible to the eye of flesh.

The possibility that they may be seen with the eye of wisdom, can be explained thus: When the lotus of the above mentioned simile is pulled out of the water, the quality of energy-packed hardness of the earth element instantaneously collapses into the sphere of weakness in momentary phases. Strength and energy deteriorate in momentary phases while weakness arises in corresponding momentary phases in the form of changed origination (*vikati-jāti*). The energy-packed water element, the cold and refreshing fire element, and the tensely bracing wind element disintegrate in momentary phases. The elements of colour (*vaṇṇa*), smell (*gandha*), taste (*rasa*), and nutrient essence (*ojā*) also disintegrate in momentary phases. If they are contemplated with concentration and wisdom, they would appear to be just like myriads of snowflakes dropping and dissolving away.

The Tremendous Speed of the Arising and Dissolution Process

The rate of change in the process of dissolution of the old material units and their replacement with new material units of the same kind in momentary phases, is so fast that it is beyond description even by drawing comparisons with such rates of change. It is also impossible to discern and differentiate between the preceding phenomenon and the succeeding one. It is not within the province of worldlings (*puthujjana*) to grasp these phenomena just with their mere intellect. They would have to contemplate the arising and dissolving process in longer momentary phases or intervals, at a rate with which they would be able to keep up. In all cases where it is beyond the capacity of the observer to keep up with the tremendous speed of the arising and dissolving process, a differentiation of discernment will not be possible, and the phenomena will appear to be one and the same (static) thing. You are advised to contemplate the sign or characteristic of the tremendous speed and frequency of change with which the process of arising and dissolution is going on in your body, as far as your observation is able to keep up with it.

If there is no process of dissolving and arising in momentary phases, there cannot be any withering away or drying up process in progressive momentary phases. So let your knowledge of insight be acute, subtle, and refined.

Seeing Innumerable Changes Innumerable Times

As shown in the example of the lotus flower there are innumerable kinds of changes going on in this body. One experiences such changes innumerable times. One sees them innumerable times. One comprehends them with knowledge and wisdom innumerable times. "Experiencing by oneself innumerable times" means the feelings associated with such exclamations as: "Oh! Something is happening inside by head. My eye, my face, my nose, my ear, the corner inside my mouth under the cheek, my lip, my mouth, my tongue, the inside of my chest, or the inside of my abdomen, are all being afflicted with this or that kind of pain or ailment." If one can contemplate the phenomena of origination, decay, and death with insight, wisdom will come within easy reach.

Knowledge, however, can hardly keep pace with the speed in the process of momentary dissolutions in primary originations (*pakati-jāti*). The point we are making is that there is not a fraction of a moment wherein a radical change in the whole of this body is not taking place by way of internal or external causes whenever conditions favourable for such change arise. The external dangers may arise from fleas, bugs, mosquitoes, vicious flies, snakes, scorpions, or from the cudgel, sword, or from calamities such as devastating fires or floods. There is no fraction of a moment wherein a radical change in the whole of the body cannot be brought about through destruction or decay. There is no fraction of a moment wherein an unpleasant origination (*aniṭṭha-jāti*) cannot take place. There is no fraction of a moment wherein destruction or ruin cannot take place. This mind-body complex, or the five aggregates (*khandha*), is endowed forever with the characteristics of momentary origination, decay, and death. Such clearly perceptible changes, destruction, and transformations can take place at the very moment of the onset of danger with a force corresponding to such an onset. Hence the expression, "This body has the characteristics of originating, decaying, and dying," contained in the seventh item of the matrix.

Here ends the exposition on the characteristic of death (maraṇa) inherent in this mind-body complex.

Eighth Item of the Matrix

The Danger of Impermanence

We have already explained many times that the constituents of this body cannot endure even for a period of a wink of an eye or a flash of lightning. If, on the other hand, it could endure for such a period it should remain unchanged even if it were struck by lightning or a thunderbolt during such a period. If that were so, the fact that it remained unchanged or unimpaired should be perceptible because the period of a wink of an eye or a flash of lightning is still long enough for an event to be perceived. Such is, however, not the case. When struck by a blow with great force, this body instantaneously transforms and changes. All such transformations and changes mean a total vanishing of the old phenomena and substitution of entirely new ones.

In this world, all water denizens and land creatures are incessantly toiling, struggling, striving, worrying, and tiring themselves out throughout every day and every hour. If the reason for this universal unrest is investigated, one will trace it to impermanence or transitoriness (*anicca*) as the greatest single factor. One will see that impermanence or transitoriness is the cause of all troubles and sufferings (*dukkha*). Then one will realize the stupendous enormity of the danger arising from impermanence or transitoriness. Were all things permanent and eternal (*nicca*), there would not be the slightest cause for striving or worrying in this world. The unavoidable performance of meritorious deeds (*puñña-kiriya*), such as almsgiving (*dāna*) and the practice of morality (*sīla*) etc., is ascribable also to impermanence or transitoriness. This practice of virtue is also a form of suffering (*dukkha*) entailing troubles and worries just on account of impermanence. Were all things in the world permanent and not impermanent, there would be no worry or anxiety for the future.

The characteristic of impermanence (*anicca-lakkhaṇa*) means continuous momentary death (*khaṇika-maraṇa*) and momentary passing away (*khaṇika-bhaṅga*). Because these momentary deaths and passing away are inherent in this mind-body complex, all sentient beings are beset by the danger of infinite troubles and worries with respect to earning a living in the present life and by infinite troubles and anxieties in the interminable round of future rebirths (*saṃsāra*).

You should, therefore, make profound your understanding and realization of this paramount problem by studying these points in conjunction with what we have said earlier about the enormity and difficulty of the task of perpetuating the life continuum, earning a living, and making investments for renewed births.

Here ends the brief exposition on the characteristic of impermanence inherent in this mind-body complex.

Ninth Item of the Matrix

The Sheer Mass of Suffering

With regard to the expression, "This physical body is a sheer mass of misery, trouble, and suffering" (*ayaṃ kāyo dukkho*), contained in the ninth item of the matrix, we should like to say that there are three kinds of suffering, namely:

1. Suffering within suffering (*dukkha-dukkha*)
2. Suffering associated with conditioning activities (*saṅkhāra-dukkha*)[14]
3. Suffering associated with radical change (*vipariṇāma-dukkha*)[15]

1. Suffering within suffering

Suffering within suffering (*dukkha-dukkha*) comprises:

1. Danger from internal sources, such as the ninety-eight kinds of diseases, entailing feelings of internal heat, pain, ache, strain, etc.
2. Danger from external sources, such as those arising from disastrous fires and floods, from weapons such as the sword or spear, from bites of poisonous snakes or scorpions, entailing pain and distress
3. The harrowing and distressing pain endured by denizens of the lower worlds of this kind of suffering

Even the sentient beings of the animal kingdom are fully aware of this kind of suffering, for when they sense approaching danger, they become seized with dread, fear, and fright. On such occasions they either scamper for cover or turn round to offer resistance, if they see fit.

Any person who has a morbid sore or ulcer on his body has reason to be afraid of the smell of burning earth oil, or earth oil, or the smell of onion or garlic fried in oil. The fear in this case is not directed to the smell itself. Instead it is directed mainly to the possible aggravation of his bodily complaint. A person who has no morbid sore on his body has nothing to fear from a frying smell. In this analogy, this mind-body complex (*khandha*) is a veritable hotbed of morbid sores and ulcers due to which it is boiling hot and in a seething turmoil. It is ever ready to be convulsed with morbid pains whenever internal and external dangers arise, which we have allegorized as "frying smell." If one has the ingenuity to investigate the source of all troubles in the shape of worries and anxieties, or dread and fear, one would trace it to this mind-body complex. It would be evident to one's intellectual knowledge that the infinite troubles and difficulties of all sentient beings are ascribable to the omnipresence of this suffering within ordinary suffering.

Here ends the brief exposition on suffering within suffering.

2. Suffering associated with conditioning activities

"Suffering associated with conditioning activities" (*saṅkhāra-dukkha*) means:

1. The preliminary suffering involved in striving with worry and anxiety to achieve the object of desire that has not yet been achieved
2. The preliminary suffering involved in striving with worry and anxiety to acquire the object of desire that has not yet been acquired
3. The preliminary suffering involved in striving with worry and anxiety to cause the arrival of the object of desire that has not yet arrived

All such masses of suffering are called "Suffering associated with conditioning activities."

3. Suffering associated with radical change

"Suffering associated with radical change" (*vipariṇāma-dukkha*) means:

1. The suffering involved in striving with worry and anxiety so that the object of one's desire, which has already been achieved after much slaving and toiling with worry and fretfulness, may not become destroyed, may not disappear, may not dwindle, may not change for the worse, may not die, may not be set upon by danger, punishment, or enmity
2. The bodily suffering (*kāyika-dukkha*) and mental suffering (*cetasika-dukkha*) sustained by one when, in spite of one's striving with worry and anxiety to prevent such destruction, disappearance, dwindling, or decline, etc., dwindling, decline, disappearance, or loss comes to pass as conditions favourable for such accidents and misfortunes arise

For a clear understanding we shall give the following simile: the three kinds of suffering are inherent in the cooked rice we eat daily. That rice burdens a person who cannot dissociate from or dispense with it in three ways. Firstly, it burdens the consumer with suffering associated with conditioning activities (*saṅkhāra-dukkha*). This involves continuous striving with worry and anxiety during the whole period between the first stage of strenuous endeavours to procure seed grains many years ahead and the last stage many years thereafter of cooking the rice for final eating. Whoever cannot dispense with eating rice is always, during this indispensable period, beset with suffering associated with conditioning activities. When, however, the eating of rice is dispensed with, one becomes liberated from such suffering. It is because rice is truly a conditioned phenomenon (*saṅkhāra-dhamma*) whose production requires an ordeal, years ahead, that there is striving with worry and anxiety to solve a formidable array of all the vexing problems involved. This is how rice burdens those who cannot give it up with suffering associated with conditioning activities.

The conditioning activities (*saṅkhāra*) described above are mere activities belonging to the concept of continuity (*santati-saṅkhāra*). As regards momentary conditioning activities (*khaṇika-saṅkhāra*) they should be considered with reference to the Law of Causal Relations, the Paṭṭhāna.

The Burden of Eating

It will now be explained how rice burdens those who cannot give up eating it with suffering associated with radical change (*vipariṇāma-dukkha*). There is a long time interval, many years, between the first stage of strenuous endeavours to secure seed grains and the final stage of solving vexing problems connected with the evacuation of waste products from the bowels after eating rice. All striving with worry and anxiety during that intervening period to avert or circumvent possible work stoppages, declines, and disasters in the production of rice, is called suffering associated with radical change in relation to rice. A person who cannot dispense with eating rice is permanently beset with suffering associated with radical change in relation to rice. When eating rice is dispensed with, he becomes liberated from such suffering. This is because all objects that are the factors of producing rice have the characteristic of destructibility and radical change whenever conditions favourable for such destruction or change arise.

All bodily and mental sufferings that arise in the course of striving with worry and anxiety, in pre-achievement and post-achievement undertakings associated with producing rice for consumption, are called suffering within ordinary suffering. Therefore, rice imposes the burden of suffering within ordinary suffering forever. Whenever conditions favourable for the destruction or loss in rice production arise, such undertakings are bound to meet with such disasters. All grief and lamentations associated with such destruction or loss constitute suffering associated with radical change, because rice has not reached the state of being cooked in an efficient process. The following misfortunes are called suffering associated with radical change because they arise only after the rice has been efficiently and successfully produced and consumed:

1. Suffering arising from a fatal case of indigestion
2. Suffering arising from various diseases (due to certain food allergies)
3. Suffering arising from evacuation of waste products of the bowels even though food has been properly digested.

There is a general saying and belief that the dissolution and destruction of dependent materiality (*upādā-rūpa*), such as colour, form (*rūpa*), smell (*gandha*), and taste (*rasa*) caused by the process of chewing or masticating inside the mouth, constitute radical change (*vipariṇāma*). All expressions used so far with respect to the Pāḷi word *vipariṇāma* are strictly in terms of the concept of continuity (*santati-paññatti*).

Here ends the description of the burdens imposed by rice on those who cannot give up eating it in the form of Suffering associated with radical change.

Radical Change in Momentary Phases

In terms of momentariness (*khaṇika*), however, the ultimate realities (*paramattha-dhamma*), such as the earth element, the water element, etc., which manifest themselves in shape or form through various originating factors (*uppāda*), cannot endure in their originally new and fresh state even for the wink of an eye. They cannot remain the same for two consecutive moments. Consumed by the fire of decay[16] (*jarā*), they are decaying and deteriorating in momentary phases. Being consumed by the fire of death[17] (*maraṇa*), they are dissolving and dying out in momentary phases.

Such momentary decays and dissolutions, due to the onslaught of the dangers of *jarā* and *maraṇa*, are called "radical change in momentary phases" (*khaṇika-vipariṇāma*). The ultimate realities (*paramattha-dhamma*), such as the earth element and the water element, that are perpetually subjected to this law of radical change in momentary phases are, indeed, the veritable burning-materials, or "food," fed to the fires of decay and death. They are not, by any means, "feasts of pleasantness." Because they are perpetually subject to the violent onslaught of decay and death, they have the characteristic of meeting horrible deaths and dissolutions, and are therefore called "the groups of suffering associated with radical change."

The Simile of the King's Dungeon with Blazing Infernos

When observed with wisdom or discernment, each of these skin-overlaid bodies, big or small, resembles a king's dungeon filled with blazing infernos. All mental and material phenomena of the body, comprising such elements as the earth element, the water element, etc., are like condemned prisoners who, by the king's orders, are to be thrown into flaming dungeons. The fires of decay and the fires of death are like the immense and highly combustible powder kegs and flaming jet devices that could blast away the whole dungeon-load of prisoners in a single blast, leaving nothing as residue.

The mode of resemblance may be explained as follows. The four great factors of life, namely:

1. Volition (*kamma*)
2. Mind or consciousness (*citta*)
3. Temperature or thermal conditions (*utu*)
4. Nutriment (*āhāra*)

which are, without a moment's interruption, forever building and creating a succession of new mental and material phenomena throughout the whole of this mind-body complex, and which are also destroying them instantaneously in the same process, are like four prison warders who are flinging the condemned prisoners down into the dungeon of raging fires without a moment's pause.

In the canonical scriptures, however, the Blessed One has, in a beautiful simile, compared the nutriment of mental volition (*mano-sañcetana-āhāra*), which is synonymous with the wholesome and unwholesome volitional actions (*kusala-akusala-kamma*), to two formidable men of great strength who are catching hold of all comers and flinging them into the pit of flames. The mental and material phenomena, which are forever arising in all parts of this mind-body complex in an uninterrupted process of momentariness, are being instantaneously blasted away into nothingness by the fires of decay and the fires of death in a similar process, leaving not even ashes as residue with each successive blast. This process of psychophysical combustion bears a resemblance, as far as complete and total dissolution is concerned, to the burning up of condemned prisoners by the immense and highly combustible fire-emitting powder kegs and flaming jet devices of the infernal dungeons, allegorized above, which leaves nothing, not even ashes, as residue after each successive blast.

Here ends the exposition on the significance of the term "radical change with momentariness."

The Troubles and Vexations of Meritorious Activities, Etc.

We now propose to compare the conditioning activities (*santati-saṅkhāra*) to rice production—as allegorized above in terms of the concept of continuity or "perceptible change" (*santati-paññatti*) within this mind-body complex, the five aggregates (*khandha*). Now, let all of you imagine your mind-body complexes, big or small, which are overlaid with skin, as a pot of rice already well-cooked.

To perpetuate your mind-body complex (which is but a succession of newly arising mental and material phenomena in an uninterrupted process from the moment of conception in a mother's womb to this moment now), you have had to undergo, during your past existences, enormous and endless trials, tribulations, and worries to earn a living, combined with doing merit. Earning a living includes such vocational activities as agriculture and trade. Meritorious deeds include giving alms, practicing morality, etc. For this purpose you have had to earn the means, accumulated with trouble. In the present existence also you have to undergo enormous and endless trials, tribulations, and worries to earn a living, combined with doing merit. Your perpetual worry and main preoccupation is to prolong, if possible, your lifetime to a hundred years counting from the moment of conception to the final indignity of death (*cuti*) of *kamma* produced materiality (*kammaja-rūpa*). All these troubles and vexations are called the mass of suffering associated with conditioning activities (*saṅkhāra-dukkha*) or with the establishment and maintenance of the five aggregates (*khandha*). If the immense never-ending task of earning a living, confronting all water denizens and land creatures at all times of the day and night, is fully realized, the immensity of the trouble of establishing and maintaining the five aggregates will also be fully realized.

In the present lifetime, one can see for oneself how much trouble is involved in giving alms or doing charity work in an organized manner. The harrowing task of collecting the wherewithal to practice charity, greeting and entertaining the receivers of alms, and discharging ancillary obligations is obvious to everybody. By judging these known facts one can form an idea as to the troubles one had taken in one's former existences as advance payment (investment) for the future well-being of the five aggregates (*khandha*). From the moment of conception in a mother's womb to the final moment of death, there is the intervening human life span. If this life span is divided into smaller divisions of time, there would be an infinite number of years, fortnights, days, hours, and moments. Now, in the course of these infinities, there is not a single moment wherein destruction cannot take place if conditions favourable for such destruction arise. Likewise, there is not a single moment in the course of these infinities wherein a change or death cannot take place if conditions favourable for such a change or death arise.

As change and death are omnipresent in this world, sentient beings in great fear, dread, fright, and anxiety try to avert and circumvent possible destruction, change, or death. All these troubles and vexations of life fall within the definition of suffering, associated with the radical change of this mind-body complex.

In spite of all efforts and strivings to avert and circumvent the dangers of approaching change or death, multifarious changes and upsets come to pass in the form of disruptions, sickness, pains, strain, aches, etc. Sentient beings have to risk those dangers and troubles for the sake of the necessities of life. There are also troubles arising out of greed, hate, conceit, and holding wrong views (*micchā-diṭṭhi*), involving, amongst other things, the practice of self-mortification by immersion in cold water during winter and subjecting one's body to the heat of fire during summer. There are also troubles and inconveniences in such spiritual pursuits as learning the Dhamma or practising the Dhamma. All these troubles come within the definition of suffering, associated with radical change of this mind-body complex. In earlier sections, we dealt with the exposition on suffering, associated with momentary change (*khaṇika-vipariṇāma-dukkha*).

In essence, the above exposition means: For a future rebirth or new origination to fit well with one's own desire, a person performs the following meritorious or demeritorious actions an hour in advance, a month in advance, a year in advance, a lifetime in advance, or world cycles in advance:

1. giving alms
2. practising morality
3. practising mind development
4. practising good conduct

5. practising evil conduct
6. becoming a monk
7. becoming a hermit
8. earning a good livelihood
9. earning a bad livelihood

All troubles, vexations, trials, and tribulations involved in all these undertakings come within the definition of suffering associated with conditioning activities (*saṅkhāra-dukkha*). The Blessed One is referring to these troubles when he proclaims (in verse no. 278 of the Dhammapada), "All conditioned things involve suffering" (*sabbe saṅkhārā dukkhā*).

As a consequence of conditioning activities performed in the past, rebirth or new origination takes place subsequently. This origination again calls for new effort and striving, with worry and anxiety, for its perpetuation and furtherance. This trouble falls within the definition of suffering associated with conditioning activities. Preparations have also been made with a view to averting and circumventing possible disruptions or breakdowns in a process of pleasurable origin (*iṭṭha-jāti*) or its being displaced by a process of unpleasurable origin (*aniṭṭha-jāti*). All these troubles taken in anticipation of the approaching danger of radical change fall within the definition of suffering associated with radical change of this mind-body complex.

Here ends the brief exposition of the characteristics and signs of suffering arising out of this mind-body complex.

Tenth Item of the Matrix

This Body is Void of a Self

We shall now explain the significance of the expression, "This body (the five aggregates) is void of a self" (*ayaṃ kāyo anattā*), contained in the tenth item of the matrix. The word "body" (*ko* in Burmese) used with reference to the Pāḷi term *anattā* does not have the same meaning as the words "physical body" in the Pāḷi terms, *kāya, sarīra, deha, tanu, vapu, gatta,* and *bondi.* The word "self", which is synonymous with the word "I", is used in everyday language to differentiate between a self as an internal entity and others as external entities. The following expressions are given as similes:

1. "In desperation, a mother will hardly regard her son as a son of herself".
2. "No one else is loved with more attachment than oneself" (*atta-sama-pemā natthi*).
3. "The son of himself. His son".
4. "The wife of himself. His wife".

In earlier chapters we have explained comprehensively the laws of nature in the ultimate sense (*dhamma-sabhāva*) insofar as they relate to the nine previous summaries or matrices. If one can realize with penetration and objective knowledge the ultimate realities in both the present and earlier summaries, the idea of a "self," "ego-entity," "sentient-being," "core," or "substance" will vanish forever and a successful breakthrough to the higher knowledge of the truth of impersonality and conditionality (*anatta-vijjā*) will be achieved. If the veil is lifted and the four great primaries, the six sense bases (*saḷāyatana*), and the six consciousness elements (*viññāṇa-dhātu*) are seen through with penetrating insight, the ego illusion (*atta-diṭṭhi*) will vanish forever. When the characteristics of impermanence (*anicca-lakkhaṇa*) and suffering (*dukkha-lakkhaṇa*) in these elements are seen through with penetrating insight, the idea of "mine," "my belongings," or "things pertaining to a self" (*attaniya*) will vanish forever. Then one reaches the goal, i.e., the end of the path leading to the higher knowledge of the Noble Ones (*ariya-vijjā*). By reaching this goal, one is delivered from the state of a mere insight trainee (*yogī*) and is transformed into one endowed with the threefold knowledge (*tevijjā*) comprising:

Knowledge of former births (*pubbe-nivāsa-ñāṇa*)
Knowledge of the divine eye (*dibba-cakkhu-ñāṇa*)
Knowledge of the extinction of all taints (*āsavakkhaya-ñāṇa*).

Epilogue

Here the concise *Vijjāmagga Dīpanī* or the *Manual of the Path to Higher Knowledge* comes to a close. It was compiled at the request of a preacher-hermit who resides within the precincts of the Kusināra Pagoda, situated on a hill near Bilin (in Thaton District) where I, a jungle recluse of the Ledi monastery near Monywa, arrived on the 4th waxing day of Nattaw in the year 1260 B.E., on a pilgrimage to pay homage. In making the request the preacher-hermit expressed the desire to know the method of overcoming the clinging to ego belief (*attavādupādāna*), which is synonymous with personality belief (*sakkāya-diṭṭhi*). This new treatise, which shows the method of winning the higher knowledge of insight (*vipassanā-vijjā*) that militates against the ego belief, was finished on the 12th waxing day of Pyatho in the year 1260 B.E. (1898 C.E.).

Here ends the Manual of the Path Leading to the Attainment of Higher Knowledge.

May this meritorious act be to me the cause of attaining Deliverance (*nibbāna paccayo hotu*).

A Short Biography of Ledi Sayādaw

Known to scholars of many countries, the Venerable Ledi Sayādaw, Aggamahāpaṇḍita, D. Litt., was perhaps the outstanding Buddhist figure of this age. With the increase in interest in Buddhism in Western lands, there is a great demand for his Buddhist discourses and writings.

Bhikkhu Ñāṇa who was later known as Ledi Sayādaw was born on Tuesday, the 13th Waxing of Nattaw, 1208 Burmese Era (1846 C.E.) at Saing-pyin Village, Dipeyin Township, Shwebo District. His parents were U Tun Tha and Daw Kyone. Early in life he was accepted into the Sangha as a *sāmaṇera* and at the age of 20 as a bhikkhu, under the patronage of Salin Sayādaw U Paṇḍicca. He received his monastic education under various teachers and later was trained in Buddhist literature by the Venerable Sankyaung Sayādaw, *Sudassana-dhaja-atulādhipati-sīripavara-mahādhamma-rājādhi-rāja-guru* of Mandalay.

He was a bright student. It was said of him: "About 2000 students attended the lectures delivered daily by the Venerable Sankyaung Sayādaw. One day the Venerable Sayādaw set in Pāḷi twenty questions on *pāramī* (perfections) and asked all the students to answer them. None of them, except Bhikkhu Ñāṇa, could answer those questions satisfactorily." He collected all these answers, and when he attained 14 rains retreats (*vassa*) and while he was still in Sankyaung Monastery, he published his first book—the *Pārami Dīpanī* (*Manual of Perfections*).

During the reign of King Theebaw he became a Pāḷi lecturer at Mahā Jotikārāma Monastery in Mandalay. A year after the capture of King Theebaw, i.e., in 1887 C.E., he moved to a place to the north of Monywa Town, where he established a monastery under the name of Ledi-tawya Monastery. He accepted many bhikkhu students from various parts of Burma and imparted Buddhist education to them. In 1897 C.E. he wrote the *Paramattha Dīpanī* (*Manual of Ultimate Truths*) in Pāḷi.

Later, he toured many parts of Burma for the purpose of propagating the Buddha Dhamma. In the towns and villages he visited, he delivered various discourses on the Dhamma and established Abhidhamma classes and Meditation Centres. He composed Abhidhamma rhymes or *abhidhamma-saṅkhitta* and taught them in his Abhidhamma classes. In some of the principle towns he spent a *vassa* (rains retreat), imparting Abhidhamma and Vinaya education to lay devotees. There are still monasteries in Burma, such as Kyaikkasan Ledi Meditation Centre in Rangoon and Leditawya Monastery, which was established by Ledi Sayādaw himself near Monywa, where his teachings and expositions are preserved and continue to be studied.

During his travels he wrote many essays, letters, poems, and manuals in Burmese. He has written more than seventy manuals (see bibliography below), of which ten have been translated into English and published in *The Light of the Dhamma* journal. The *Vipassanā Dīpanī* (*Manual of Insight*) was translated by his disciple Sayādaw U Ñāṇa, Paṭhamagyaw. The *Paṭṭhānuddesa Dīpanī* (*A Concise Exposition of the Buddhist Philosophy of Relations*)[18] was originally written in Pāḷi by the late Ledi Sayādaw and translated by Sayādaw U Ñāṇa. The *Niyāma Dīpanī* (*Manual of Cosmic Order*) was translated by U Ñāṇa and Dr. Barua and edited by Mrs. Rhys Davids. The *Sammādiṭṭhi Dīpanī* (*Manual of Right Understanding*), the *Catusacca Dīpanī* (*Manual of the Four Noble Truths*), and the *Alin-Kyan* (*An Exposition of Five Kinds of Light*), translated in part only, were all translated by the editors of *The Light of the Dhamma*. *Bodhipakkhiya Dīpanī* (*Manual of the Factors Leading to Enlightenment*) was translated by U Sein Nyo Tun, I.C.S. (Retd.), and the *Maggaṅga Dīpanī* (*Manual of the Constituents of the Noble Path*) was translated by U Saw Tun Teik, B.A., B.L., and revised and edited by the English Editorial Board of the Union Buddha Sāsana Council. *Ānapāna Dīpanī* (Manual of Breathing) was translated by U Sein Nyo Tun and the *Vijjāmagga Dīpanī* (Manual of the Path to Higher Knowledge) was translated by U Pu, Retired Assistant Secretary, Ministry of Labour—Burma.

In the year 1910, while residing at the Masoyain Monastery in Mandalay, the Venerable Ledi Sayādaw, together with the *Abhidhaja-mahāraṭṭhaguru* Masoyain Sayādaw of Mandalay (President of the Sixth great Buddhist Council), the Venerable Sayādaw U Ñāṇa, and U Shwe Zan Aung B.A., founded the Burma Buddhist Foreign Mission. This project was carried on by the Masoyain Sayādaw of Mandalay until the death of his English-educated colleague in this undertaking, the Sayādaw U Ñāṇa, who died ca. 1936.

Ledi Sayadaw was awarded the title of *Aggamahāpaṇḍita* by the Government of India in 1911 C.E. Later, the University of Rangoon conferred on him the degree of D. Litt. (*Honoris Causa*). In his last years he settled down at Pyinmana where he died in 1923 C.E. at the ripe old age of 77.

It is well known that in 1856 King Mindon (1852–1877) conceived the meritorious idea of having the Pāḷi Tipiṭaka carved on 729 marble slabs in Maṇḍalay so that the Teaching might be preserved. The work took place from 1860 to 1868. It is not so well known outside Burma, however, that a similar mark of respect for the works of Venerable Ledi Sayādaw was made by his supporters in Monywa in Upper Burma after his death. This recognition and treatment of a Buddhist monk's works is unique and it gives some indication of the immense importance attached to his writings.

The reputation of Ledi Sayādaw still lives on in Burma and in the Buddhist world. He was a bhikkhu of great learning and a prolific writer with a unique style of exposition. He was an austere bhikkhu, yet a very humane one, who would often write a whole treatise or a long letter in reply to a question asked by a student or listener.

End Notes

1 U Tin U rendered this term in three ways in this section: "knowledge of *kamma* ownership," "knowledge in seeing that all beings have *kamma* as their own property," and "knowledge of *kamma* as one's own property." In the (sub-) commentaries the term is explained thus, "*kammassakatāñāṇa*: 'this is his own *kamma*,' his state is due to '*kamma*-ownership.' The knowledge about it, 'this *kamma* is the own property of beings; this is our own property,' is such knowing-knowledge." In the subcommentary on the Majjhima Nikāya it is explained as: *kammassakatāñāṇan-ti kammaṃ sako etassāti kammassako, tassa bhāvo kammassakatā, tattha ñāṇaṃ idaṃ kammaṃ sattānaṃ sakaṃ, idaṃ no sakanti evaṃ jānanañāṇaṃ.*

2 *Vavatthāna* means "definition" or "analysis." *Dhammavavatthāna* could also be translated as "knowledge (arising out) of the analysis of the Dhamma."

3 The *cūḷasotāpanna* literally means "lesser stream-enterer," see *Visuddhimagga* XIX.27, translated in *The Path of Purification.*

4 An idiom based on Indian and Burmese Buddhist mythology that Ledi Sayādaw often uses to indicate the symbolically most important physical phenomena in this world. Mount Meru is the highest mountain at the center of Jambudīpa and the universe. The four rivers including the Ganges flow from its four sides, which are occupied by the four regent gods. Mount Cakkavāḷa, or the "circumjacent mountains," is a mythical range of mountains encircling the earth and the limit of light and darkness. The Great Earth is the wide world, the earth.

5 *Ākāsa* (space) is a permanent concept (*nicca paññatti*), a subjective element which has no objective reality.

The above remark probably was made by Sayādaw U Ñāṇika. In the *Manual of Insight* (*Vipassanā Dīpanī*), Wheel 31/32, there is a similar footnote by Sayādaw U Ñāṇika. Following this note, Venerable Ñāṇaponika Thera makes the following remark about the permanent concept doctrine, which seems to be particular to the Ledi Sayādaw school, and perhaps arose under the influence of Ledi Sayādaw's studies of Western, in particular Platonic, philosophy:

"The statement of the translator, the Venerable U Ñāṇa, ascribing the teaching on the "eternal nature" of concepts and space to Buddhist philosophy in general, requires qualification. This teaching is obviously of late origin, being found neither in the Abhidhamma Piṭaka nor in the old Abhidhamma commentaries. The earliest reference might be in the Parivāra, a late summary of the Vinaya, appended as the last book to the Vinaya Piṭaka. There, in a stanza, it is said that "all formations (*saṅkhārā*) are impermanent, painful, not-self and conditioned (*saṅkhata*); Nibbāna and space are not-self"—which, by implication, may mean that the latter two (which do not include concept) are unconditioned (*asaṅkhata*). It was characteristic of the later schools (also the Śrāvakayāna school of the Vaibhāṣikas) to have enlarged the list of the *asaṅkhata-dhammā*, while the Dhammasaṅgaṇi (and so also the Sutta Piṭaka) speaks only of Nibbāna as unconditioned (*asaṅkhata*). It is also significant that the two Abhidhamma manuals, *Abhidhammatthasaṅgaha* and *Abhidhammāvatāra*, both have chapters on concept (*paññatti*), but make no mention of its eternal and unconditioned nature." (BPS editor)

6 (i) "Thought-conception (*vitakka*) is the laying hold of thought, giving it attention. Its characteristic consists in fixing consciousness to the object" (*Buddhist Dictionary*, Nyanatiloka, Colombo, Sri Lanka, 1950), Ed. (ii) The understanding of *vitakka* depends on whether it is taken literally in the strict sense, which is supramundane, or in common usage, which is mundane. In commentaries, such as the *Visuddhimagga*, *Aṭṭhasālinī*, and *Abhidhammatthavibhāvanī*, the common characteristic of *vitakka* is: "*cetaso abhiniropaṇalakkhaṇa*" (directing and lifting the *citta* and *cetasikas* toward the objects). In the higher states of mind, *vitakka* serves as an initial application, lifting *citta* up toward wisdom, which, in the case of path and fruition (*magga-phala*), is conducive to extirpation of defilements, and directing citta toward ecstatic concentration (*appaṇā-samādhi*), which, in the case of jhāna or sublime (*mahaggata*) fields, is capable of overcoming the hindrances.

In common usage, however, *vitakka* means applied or speculative thought, thinking about various aspects of divergent objects (*nānāppakāraparikappana*), or, to put it simply, daydreaming. As regards temperaments, *vitakka*, as one type of *cariyā*, called "speculative temperament," is explained in detail in *The Path of Purification* (pp. 102-112). In the Burmese version of the present text, Ledi Sayādaw is using *vitakka* in this sense, so "random thought" or "idle thought" is correct. I do not think that "simply wool-gathering" is a suitable expression to convey this idea. (Ven. Sayādaw U Nyanika).

There is an extensive explanation regarding *cetasika*, especially *vitakka*, in *Compendium of Philosophy* (*Abhidhammatthasaṅgaha*), translated by U Shwe Zan Aung, B.A. (P.T.S., 1910, pp. 238 ff.)

7 *Cakkhu-rūpena ca saṃvāsā rāgaputtaṃ vijāyati.* (*Caturārakkha-dīpanī* v. 74.)

8 The *bhavaṅga* can take one of three objects, but in any individual life it always has the same object on every occasion of *bhavaṅga-citta*. The three objects are: (1) the *kamma* itself (*kamma*), that is, an image of the deed itself being performed; (2) the sign of *kamma* (*kamma-nimitta*), an image of some object associated with the deed, such as a dagger in the case of a murderer or a dagoba in the case of a pious lay devotee who often went to the temples to worship; or (3) the sign of the destination (*gati-nimitta*). The last is some sign connected with the future destiny that appeared to the death consciousness of the preceding existence; for example, a terrible fire in the case of a rebirth in one of the hot hells, or a heavenly mansion in the case of a deva rebirth. This sign becomes the object of the *paṭisandhi-citta* (rebirth-linking consciousness) and *bhavaṅga-citta* of the current existence. (Editor)

9 But see Bhikkhu Ñāṇamoli's assessment of this term "name and form" (*nāma-rūpa*) at Appendix I, p. 330 *Minor Readings & Illustrator* (*Khuddakapāṭha*) P.T.S.

10 The eight attainments (*samāpatti*) are:

1. The first mental absorption (*paṭhama-jhāna*)
2. The second mental absorption (*dutiya-jhāna*)
3. The third mental absorption (*tatiya-jhāna*)
4. The fourth mental absorption (*catuttha-jhāna*)
5. The sphere of unbounded space (*ākāsānañcāyatana*)
6. The sphere of unbounded consciousness (*viññāṇañcāyatana*)
7. The sphere of nothingness (*ākiñcaññāyatana*)
8. The sphere of neither-perception-nor-non-perception (*nevasaññānāsaññāyatana*).

11 The ten stages of insight knowledge are:

1. Insight into the three characteristics of existence (*sammasana-ñāṇa*)
2. Insight into the process of arising and dissolution of phenomena (*udayabbaya-ñāṇa*)

3. Insight into the process of dissolution of phenomena (*bhaṅga-ñāṇa*)
4. Insight into the fearful condition of phenomena (*bhaya-ñāṇa*)
5. Insight into the fault-riddenness of phenomena (*ādīnava-ñāṇa*)
6. Insight arising from the wearisome condition of phenomena (*nibbidā-ñāṇa*)
7. Insight arising from a yearning for escape (*muccitu-kamyatā-ñāṇa*)
8. Insight arising from reflective contemplation (*paṭisaṅkhā-ñāṇa*)
9. Insight arising from equanimity (*saṅkhār'upekkhā-ñāṇa*)
10. Insight knowledge of adaptation (*anuloma-ñāṇa*)

12 See End Note 4.

13 The six seasons according to ancient Indian notions are: *hemanta, sisira, vasanta, gimha, vassāna,* and *sarada,* approximately equivalent to December and January, February and March, April and May, June and July, August and September, and October and November.

14 U Pu (or Stanley Davidson) rendered this term here as "pre-achievement suffering," which does not sufficiently convey the meaning of this important Pali term, therefore it has been changed to the more appropriate translation that U Pu used in later sections of this chapter. (BPS editor)

15 The translation here was "post-achievement suffering," which has been changed to the better rendering used in later sections. (BPS Editor)

16 See Preface, last paragraph.

17 See Preface, last paragraph.

18 Published under the title *The Buddhist Philosophy of Relations* (Wheel 331/333) by the B.P.S., Kandy.

Bibliography of Ledi Sayādaw

Below are some of the *ṭīkās*, manuals, essays, and letters written by the Venerable Ledi Sayādaw.

In Pāli

Anattavibhāvanā (Explanation of Not Self)
Aṇu-Dīpanī (Manual of Atoms)
Exposition of Buddhism for the West
London Pāḷi Devi Pucchā Visajjanā (Questions and Answers by the Pāḷi Lady in London [i.e., Mrs. Rhys Davids])
Nirutti Dīpanī (Manual of Philology) or *Vuttimoggallāna Ṭīkā* (Subcommentary on the "Gloss of the Moggallāna Grammar")
Niyāma Dīpanī (Manual of Cosmic Order)*
Padhāna Sutta (Sutta on Putting Forth Effort [Pāḷi and word for word meanings])
Paramattha Dīpanī (Manual of Ultimate Truths) or *Abhidhammatthasaṅgaha Mahā Ṭīkā* (Great Subcommentary on the Comprehensive Manual of Abhidhamma)
Paṭṭhānuddesa Dīpanī (Manual of Conditional Relations)* °
Sammādiṭṭhi Dīpanī (Manual of Right View)*
Sāsanasampatti Dīpanī (Manual of Success in the Dispensation)
Sāsanavipatti Dīpanī (Manual of Regress in the Dispensation)
Vaccavācaka Ṭīkā (Subcommentary on Reciting/Teaching Words)
Vibhatyattha Ṭīkā (Subcommentary on Inflection)
Vipassanā Dīpanī (Manual of Insight)* °
Yamaka Pucchā Visajjanā (Questions and Answers on the Book of Relations)

In Burmese

Āhāra Dīpanī (Manual of Nutritive Essence)
Alaṅkāra Saṅkhitta (Brief Manual of Prosody)
Alin-kyan (Manual of the Five Kinds of Light)* °
Ānapāna Dīpanī (Manual of Breathing)°
Anatta Dīpanī (Manual of Not Self)
Asaṅkhāra-Sasaṅkhāra-vinicchaya Dīpanī (Manual of the Decision on the Conditioned and Unconditioned)
Bhāvanā Dīpanī (Manual of Mental Development)

Bodhipakkhiya Dīpanī (Manual of the Factors Leading to Enlightenment)*
Catusacca Dīpanī (Manual of the Four Noble Truths)*
Cetiyaṅgaṇa-vinicchaya Dīpanī (Manual of the Decision on the Factors of the Stupa)
Dānādi Dīpanī (Manual of Generosity, etc.)
Ājīvaṭṭhamaka Sīla Vinicchaya (Decision on the Eight Precepts)
Vikālabhojana-sikkhāpada Vinicchaya (Decision on the Training Rule of Eating at the Wrong Time)
Dhamma Dīpanī (Manual of Dhamma)
Dīghāsana-vinicchaya Dīpanī (Manual of the Decision on Long Seats)
Gambhīra-kabyā-kyan (Manual of Profound Verses)
Goṇasurā Dīpanī (Manual of Cows and Alcohol)
Iṇaparibhoga-vinicchaya Dīpanī (Manual of the Decision on Debt and Wealth)
Kammaṭṭhāna Dīpanī (Manual of Meditation Subjects)
Lakkhaṇa Dīpanī (Manual of Characteristics of Existence)
Ledi Pucchā-visajjanā (Questions and Answers of Ledi Sayādaw)
Maggaṅga Dīpanī (Manual of the Constituents of the Noble Path)* °
Mahāsayana Dīpanī (Manual of the Great Seat)
Nibbāna Dīpanī (Manual of Nibbāna)
Nibbāna-pucchā-visajjanā Dīpanī (Manual with Questions and Answers on Nibbāna)
Niyāma Dīpanī (Manual of Cosmic Order)
Paramattha Saṅkhitta (Brief Manual of Ultimate Reality)
Pāramī Dīpanī (Manual of Perfections)
Paṭiccasamuppāda Dīpanī (Manual of Dependent Origination)
Rūpa-Saṅkhitta (Brief Manual of Material Qualities)
Sotāpanna-pucchā-visajjanā (Answers on the Stream-Enterer)
Rogantara Dīpanī (Manual of the Disappearance of Disease)
Rūpa Dīpanī (Manual of Material Qualities)
Saccattha Dīpanī (Manual of the Meaning of Truth)
Sadda Saṅkhitta (Brief Manual of Words)
Saraṇagamaṇa-vinicchaya Dīpanī (Manual of the Decision on Going for Refuge)
Sāsanadāyajja Dīpanī (Manual of the Inheritance of the Dispensation)
Sāsanavisodhanī Vols. I, II & III (The Purifier of the Dispensation)
Sikkhā-gahana-vinicchaya Dīpanī (Manual of the Decision on the

Taking on of the Training Rules)
Sīlavinicchaya Dīpanī (Manual of the Decision on Virtue)
Somanassa-upekkhā Dīpanī (Manual of Joy and Equanimity)
Sukumāra Dīpanī (Manual of the Delicate)
Upasampadā-vinicchaya Dīpanī (Manual of the Decision on the Higher Acceptance into the Saṅgha)
Uttamapurisa Dīpanī (Manual of the Excellent Man)°
Vijjāmagga Dīpanī (Manual of the Path to Higher Knowledge)°
Vinaya Saṅkhitta (Brief Manual on Discipline)
Virati-sīlavinicchaya Dīpanī (Manual of the Decision on the Virtue of Abstinence)
Admonitory letter prohibiting Lotteries and Gambling
Admonitory letter to the inhabitants of Dipeyin Township for abstention from taking intoxicants
Admonitory letter to U Saing, headman of Saingpyin Village for abstention from taking intoxicants
An Advice to hold a Lighting Festival at the Bo Tree within the precincts of Ledi Monastery, Monywa
Brief Manual on Spelling
Brief Manual on Alphabets
Inscription at Sīhataw Pagoda, written by the Ledi Sayādaw at the request of U Hmat
Letter of reply to U Ba Bwa, Township Officer of Dedaye, saying that he could not go on a pilgrimage to Ceylon that year
Letter to U Hmat, a Ruby Merchant of Mogok
Open letter for abstention from taking beef
Verses on Saṃvega

The English translations of the works marked (*) are printed in a single volume: *The Manuals of Buddhism* published by The Deputy Director, at the Religious Affairs Dept. Press, Yegu, Kabā-Aye P.O., Rangoon, Burma and the Vipassana Research Institute, Igatpuri, India.

The works marked (°) are (also) published by the BPS.

ABOUT PARIYATTI

Pariyatti is dedicated to providing affordable access to authentic teachings of the Buddha about the Dhamma theory (*pariyatti*) and practice (*paṭipatti*) of Vipassana meditation. A 501(c)(3) nonprofit charitable organization since 2002, Pariyatti is sustained by contributions from individuals who appreciate and want to share the incalculable value of the Dhamma teachings. We invite you to visit www.pariyatti.org to learn about our programs, services, and ways to support publishing and other undertakings.

Pariyatti Publishing Imprints

Vipassana Research Publications (focus on Vipassana as taught by S.N. Goenka in the tradition of Sayagyi U Ba Khin)

BPS Pariyatti Editions (selected titles from the Buddhist Publication Society, copublished by Pariyatti)

MPA Pariyatti Editions (selected titles from the Myanmar Pitaka Association, copublished by Pariyatti)

Pariyatti Digital Editions (audio and video titles, including discourses)

Pariyatti Press (classic titles returned to print and inspirational writing by contemporary authors)

Pariyatti enriches the world by

- disseminating the words of the Buddha,
- providing sustenance for the seeker's journey,
- illuminating the meditator's path.

www.ingramcontent.com/pod-product-compliance
Lightning Source LLC
Chambersburg PA
CBHW031958040426
42448CB00006B/410
* 9 7 8 1 6 8 1 7 2 3 0 2 0 *